THE BEST OF GREAT BRITAIN

A Journey Filled with Discovery and Adventure

Great Britain Travel Guides

Disclaimer

The content of this book has been checked and compiled with great care. However, no guarantee or guarantee can be taken over for the contents' completeness, correctness, and topicality. The content of this book represents the personal experience and opinion of the author and is for entertainment purposes only. The content should not be confused with medical help.

There will be no legal responsibility or liability for damages resulting from counterproductive exercise or errors by the reader. Furthermore, no guarantee can be given for success. The author, therefore, assumes no responsibility for the non-achievement of the goals described in the book.

Contents

CHAPTER 1: INTRODUCTION TO THE UNITED KINGDOM

The word "United Kingdom" is commonly used to refer to the island of Great Britain or England, Scotland, and Wales as a political unit. It is occasionally used interchangeably with the term "Great Britain." The term "United Kingdom" has been used to refer to Great Britain's former kingdom, even though the official name was just "Great Britain" from 1707 to 1800.

In 1801, the 1800 Union Acts formed the Merged Kingdom of Great Britain and Ireland, thereby uniting the kingdoms of Great Britain and Ireland. The country became known as the "United Kingdom " after the partition of Ireland and the establishment of the Irish State, which took place in 1922. Over several hundred years, a succession of annexations, unions, and separations of constituent countries led to the United Kingdom's formation.

When the United Kingdom and Ireland joined the Kingdom of Ireland in 1801, the United Kingdom and Ireland were born. Most of Ireland seceded from the United Kingdom in 1922, resulting in the formation of the modern United Kingdom in 1927.

The United Kingdom is positioned in the northwest region of Europe, off the north-western coast of the continent. The British Isles are made up of the island of Great Britain, the northern part of the island of Ireland, and a slew of smaller islands. A land border separates Northern Ireland and the Republic of Ireland. The United Kingdom, which has the world's 12th-longest coastline, is surrounded by the Atlantic Ocean. To the east lies the North Sea, to the south is the English Channel, and to the west is the Celtic Sea. The Irish Sea separates Great Britain and Ireland.

In 2020, the United Kingdom had a land area of 93,628 square miles and approximately 67 million people.

England, Scotland, Wales, and Northern Ireland are all referred to as distinct nations even though the United Kingdom is a sovereign state Scotland, Wales, and Northern Ireland are referred to as "regions" in some statistical summaries, such as those for the United Kingdom's twelve NUTS 1 region. Northern Ireland is also referred to as a "province." Northern Ireland's time is described as "contentious," with "choices sometimes betraying one's political ideals."

The United Kingdom is a unitary parliamentary democracy with a constitutional monarchy. Since 1952, Queen Elizabeth II has served as the country's head and monarch. The United Kingdom comprises four countries: England, Scotland, Wales, and Northern Ireland. Except for England, each component country has its sovereign government with various powers. After a vote in 2016, the UK stayed in the European Communities (EC) and its successor, the European Union (EU), from 1973 until 2020.

This country is Europe's fourth-largest, the Commonwealth's fifth-largest, and the world's 22nd-largest. Net long-term foreign migration contributed more to the population increase in mid-2014 and mid-2015. Between 2001 and 2011, United Kingdom's population increased at a 0.7 per cent annual rate. According to the 2011 census, the proportion of people aged 0–14 years old has dropped from 31% to 18%, while people aged 65 and more have increased from 5% to 16%. In 2018, the United Kingdom's population was 41.7 years old.

England has a population of 53 million people as of 2011, accounting for roughly 84 per cent of the UK's total population. As a result, England has become one of the world's densely populated countries, with 420 people per square kilometre in mid-2015, with most of the population concentrated in London and the southeast. According to the 2011 census, Scotland's population was 5.3 million, Wales's 3.06 million, and Northern Ireland's 1.81 million.

1.1 Information about the geography of the UK

Celtic broadleaf woods, English Lowlands beech forests, North Atlantic damp mixed forests, and Caledon conifer forests are the four terrestrial ecoregions found in the United Kingdom. The country was ranked 161st out of 172 countries in the 2019 Forest Landscape Integrity Index, with a mean score of 1.65/10.

A location map of the United Kingdom shows that it is located between 49 and 61 degrees north latitude and 9 and 2 degrees east longitude. The United Kingdom's coastline stretches over 11,073 miles (17,820 kilometres). The world's longest underwater tunnel at 31 miles, the Channel Tunnel connects it to mainland Europe.

1.2 Culture and language

Across the United Kingdom, there is a wide range of ethnic varieties. According to the 2001 census, ethnic minorities made up 30.4 per cent of London's population and 37.4 per cent of Leicester's population in 2005. Discrimination against individuals based on their race is illegal, religion, gender, sexuality, or handicap in the United Kingdom; this has helped provide habitation and settlement for diverse people worldwide.

Several elements have influenced the United Kingdom's culture, notably its island location and its position as a unified state of four nations, each with its customs, practices, and symbolism. Historically, many former British colonies have retained British influence in their languages and cultures as a legacy of the British Empire; this common culture is referred to today as the Anglosphere. These former British colonies include countries such as Australia, Canada, India, Ireland, New Zealand, Pakistan, South Africa, and the United States.

Due to its tremendous cultural influence, the United Kingdom has been termed a "cultural powerhouse." As a result, the United Kingdom was named the third most positively perceived nation in a global opinion poll in 2013 and 2014.

The United Kingdom enjoys a lovely ceremony, and royal weddings are no exception. Royal marriages are observed as national holidays. The most recent significant event was Prince William's marriage to Catherine Middleton in 2011. Their wedding day was proclaimed a national holiday, giving them an extra day off.

English is the official spoken language of the United Kingdom.

Ninety-five per cent of the UK's population is monolingual English speakers, with 5.5 per cent speaking languages that recent immigration brought to the UK. Urdu, Bengali, Sylheti, Hindi, and Gujarati are among the most common South Asian languages. Polish is the second-largest language spoken in England, with 546,000 speakers, according to the 2011 census. Three-quarters of a million people spoke little or no English in 2019.

Although the UK has a variety of regional accents, visitors should not be concerned because UK natives always speak clearly for students, and local accents are helpful and friendly. Since English is a globally recognized and spoken language, it is easier for visitors to understand different English accents from all over the UK.

Currently, the British government recognises four Celtic languages as being functional. Irish Gaelic, Welsh, Scottish Gaelic, and Breton are the four languages. Three indigenous Celtic languages spoken in the United Kingdom are Welsh, Irish, and Scottish Gaelic. Breton is restored as a first language after going extinct in the late 1800s. It has a tiny community of second language speakers.

According to the 2011 Census, Welsh is spoken by around one-fifth of Wales's population. Furthermore, there are an estimated 200,000 Welsh speakers in the United Kingdom. Due to a lack of particular protection and promotion obligations, Scots, a language originating from early northern Middle English, has limited recognition in Northern Ireland alongside its regional variation, Ulster-Scots.

Students in England are required to study a second language until they reach the age of fourteen. French and German are the most often taught second languages in England and Scotland. Welsh is taught as a second language or first language to pupils in Wales under 16.

1.3 Status of religion

Christianity is the widely practised faith in the United Kingdom, with 71.6 per cent of all respondents identifying as Christians in the 2001 census, followed by Islam (2.8 per cent), Hinduism (1.0 per cent), Sikhism (0.6 per cent), Judaism (0.5 per cent), Buddhism (0.3 per cent), and all other religions (0.3 per cent).

The Church of England is the established church in England. The British monarch acts as its Supreme Governor, and it has a seat in the British Parliament. Scotland's national church is known as the Church of Scotland. The monarch of the United Kingdom is a regular member. Upon their accession, the monarch must swear an oath to "keep and protect the Protestant Religion and Presbyterian Church Government". The Church of Wales was liquidated in 1920, before Ireland's partition. Anglicans make up 62 per cent of Christians, Catholics 13.5 per cent, Presbyterians 6%, Methodists 3.4 per cent, and other Protestant faiths, including Plymouth Brethren and Orthodox churches, account for small percentages.

1.4 Economy and health

Healthcare is a devolved topic in the United Kingdom, with each county having its own private and publicly funded healthcare system. All people who live in the UK have access to public healthcare; taxes have paid primarily free. The United Kingdom's healthcare system was named fifteenth best in Europe and eighteenth best globally by the World Health Organization in 2000.

Since 1979, the amount spent on healthcare has climbed considerably. The United Kingdom spends 8.4% of its GDP on healthcare.

In the United Kingdom, governmental and non-governmental medical regulating organizations include the General Medical Council, the Royal College, and the Nursing and Midwifery Council. The United Kingdom Government, Northern Ireland Executive, the Scottish Government, and the Welsh Government are all responsible for healthcare. In England, the UK Government is in charge of healthcare; in Northern Ireland, the Northern Ireland Executive is in order of healthcare; and in Scotland, the Scottish Government is in cost of healthcare. There are disparities in each National Health Service's policies and priorities, resulting in contrasts.

The United Kingdom has the fifth-largest gross domestic product (GDP), the eighth-largest purchasing power economy, a high-income economy, and the third-highest human development index globally. During the 19th and 20th centuries, the United Kingdom was the most affluent country globally as it was the first country to become industrialized. The United Kingdom remains one of the world's great powers, with considerable economic, cultural, military, scientific, technical, and political significance. It is a recognized nuclear power with an army budget ranking fourth.

The pound (£) is The United Kingdom's currency.

ATMs are widely available and usually free to use. You can pay for products and services almost anywhere in the UK using a debit or credit card. Small stores, outdoor markets, pubs and cafes, local buses, and taxis frequently require cash.

The Airbus A380's engines and wings are made in the United Kingdom.

BAE Systems is a crucial player in some of the most critical defence aerospace projects globally. Significant elements of the

Typhoon Euro fighter are manufactured in the United Kingdom, and the planes are assembled for the Royal Air Force. The country also manufactures a range of parts for the F35 Joint Strike Fighter, the world's largest single defence project. Airbus UK also manufactures the A400 m military transporter's wings. Rolls-Royce is the world's second-largest aircraft engine manufacturer, with over 30,000 machines in use in the civil and military sectors. Its engines are used in over 30 distinct commercial aircraft types.

With an annual sale of almost £30 billion, the UK aviation industry is the world's second or third-largest international aircraft industry, depending on the measurement method.

London, Britain's capital and megacity, with a population of 14 million people, is a global city and economic centre. Other notable cities include Birmingham, Manchester, Glasgow, Liverpool, and Leeds. The United Kingdom has plenty of coal, zinc, gold, potash, limestone, silica sand, chalk, petroleum, natural gas, iron ore gypsum, and arable land.

1.6 What can we expect from the weather in the UK?

The United Kingdom is ranked 4th out of 180 countries on the Environmental Performance Index. A law has been passed requiring the UK to achieve zero greenhouse gas emissions by 2050. The United Kingdom has a mild climate; This means that Britain experiences cool, rainy winters and warm, rainy summers. It is rarely subjected to the extremes of heat or cold, drought, or wind found in other regions. Because not all parts of the UK have the same climate, weather conditions are also quite variable. London has a warm and dry climate in the summer.

The majority of the United Kingdom has a moderate climate, with consistently cool temperatures and plenty of rain. The temperature changes with the seasons, rarely falling below 0 degrees Celsius (32 degrees Fahrenheit) or over 30 degrees Celsius (86 degrees Fahrenheit). Scotland's higher elevations have a continental subarctic climate, whereas the mountains have a tundra environment. Although the eastern areas are mainly unaffected by this wind, the rain falls over the western regions and the driest eastern parts. The Gulf Stream warms Atlantic currents, resulting in moderate winters, particularly in the west, where winters are moist and even more so on high ground. Summers in England are hottest in the southeast and coldest in the north. Snowfall can be heavy on high ground in the winter and early spring, and it can sometimes settle to a considerable depth away from the hills.

On the Köppen climatic classification system, the United Kingdom's climate is classified as an oceanic climate, dominant in most of north-western Europe.

The Atlantic Ocean and latitude have an impact on regional climates.

The proximity of the UK to the Atlantic Ocean, Northern Ireland, Wales, and the western sections of England and Scotland are, as a result, often the warmest, coolest, and windiest regions of the country, with intermediate temperatures that are rarely extreme. There is less wind and rain towards the east, although the temperature varies significantly throughout the year and the day. Northern places are typically more comfortable and wetter than southern areas, with slightly greater temperature swings.

The United Kingdom traverses the higher mid-latitudes between 49° and 61°N on Europe's western shore. Pressure changes and unsettled weather are common in the UK since it is always in or near the path of the polar front jet stream. It's possible to experience different weather conditions on the same day. In the United Kingdom, the weather is typically cool, cloudy, and wet. Temperatures exceeding 90°F are unusual.

Northern Ireland and the west of Scotland are more exposed to the maritime polar air mass, which provides warm, damp wind; the continental polar air mass, which brings cold, dry air, is more exposed in Eastern Scotland and England's north-east. In the summer, continental tropical air masses from the south bring warm, dry air to the south and southeast of England, the least exposed to polar air masses from the northwest. The usual temperature is between 18 and 25 degrees Celsius.

In summer, when the air masses are firm in their respective areas, there can be a significant temperature difference between the far north of Scotland (including its islands) and the southeast of England – often a difference of 10-15 °C (18-27 °F), but occasionally as much as 20 °C (36 °F) or more. The Northern Isles can reach temperatures of 15 °C (59 °F) in the summer, while Cambridge in the East of England came to 38.7 °C (101.7 °F) on July 25, 2019.

It takes 1339.7 hours of sunshine every year in the United Kingdom, slightly less than 30% of the maximum amount possible in a year. The overall number of hours spent in the sun varies between 1200 to 1580 per year, with the UK receiving more sunlight since 1996.

Due to its high latitude and oceanic regulated climate, the United Kingdom has foggy skies. The country's northern regions get the fewest sunshine hours, whereas the southern parts and the southern coast of England have the most. The sunniest places are the counties of Dorset, Hampshire, Sussex, and Kent, which have yearly average totals of roughly 1,750 hours of sunshine each year.

Northern, western, and highland portions of the UK are often cloudier, with some mountainous places having fewer than 1,000 hours of sunlight each year.

In contrast to lowland places, valley locations like the South Wales Valleys get less sunshine because of the mountains that provide shelter and light in the morning and evening. The mountains of Wales, northern England, and Scotland can be very foggy and misty. Sea fog can form near the coast in the spring and early summer. Radiation fog can form over inland portions of the United Kingdom in the winter and last long hours, posing a severe threat to cars and aircraft.

Blocking anticyclones may occasionally pass across the United Kingdom, lasting weeks or months. However, clear skies and few clouds are typical because of the subsided, dry air, resulting in chilly evenings and sunny days in the summer.

The mountainous northwest of England has cooler temperatures and more rainfall throughout the year.

The United Kingdom's climate is classified into four main regions:
Winters in the southeast are bitterly cold, and summers are scorching and dry.

The southwest's winters are mild and moist, while the summers are warm and muggy.

The Pacific Northwest has moderate winters, cool summers, and plenty of rain throughout the year.

The northeast features a harsh winter, a scorching summer, and rain all year.

It is customary in London for summers to be brief, pleasant, and partially cloudy. On the other hand, Winters are long, severely cold, windy, and mostly gloomy. Throughout the year, the temperature in the United Kingdom fluctuates from 39°F to 74°F, with temperatures rarely falling below 30°F or going over 84°F.

The warm season runs for around two months, from June 15 to September 7, with daily high temperatures averaging about 69°F. July is London's hottest month, with average highs of 73°F and lows of 59°F. The extraordinary season lasts 4.0 months, from November 16 to March 18, with daily average temperatures of less than 53°F. With an average low of 39°F and a high of 48°F, February is the snowiest in London.

The clearer season in London starts on April 2 and extends for around 6.5 months, ending on October 20. July is the clearest month in London, with the sky being clear, mostly clear, or partly cloudy 57% of the time. Approximately October 20 marks the beginning of the rainy season, which lasts 5.4 months and ends approximately April 2. December is the cloudiest month in London, with the sky being overcast or primarily gloomy at 72 per cent.

In London, the likelihood of heavy rains varies throughout the year. The wetter season lasts 8.2 months, from May 27 to February 5, with a greater than 26% chance of rain on any given day. The wettest month in London is November, with an average of 9 days of rain. According to this categorisation, rain is the most common precipitation throughout the year, with a peak probability of 32 per cent on December 30. October is the wettest month in the UK, with a higher likelihood of heavy rain.

Gales, defined as winds of 51 to 101 kilometres per hour, are strongly linked to the passage of deep depressions across the country. The Hebrides have 35 days of gale every year, whereas inland locations in England and Wales have less than five days. Wind speeds are more potent at higher heights than at lower elevations, and Great Dun Fell in Cumbria averaged 114 days of gale per year from 1963 to 1976. On December 15, 1979, the highest gust recorded at a low level in England was 191 km/h at Gwen nap Head in Cornwall, and on October 16, 1987, a 115-mph gust was recorded Shoreham-By-Sea. From February 5 to May 27, the drier season lasts 3.7 months. April has the fewest rainy days in London, with an average of 6.5 days with at least 0.04 inches of rainfall.

Since the dew point doesn't change as quickly as the temperature, the temperature may drop at night. In London, when the humidity is too high to be comfortable, the amount of time is not very different from year to year. It stays at about 0% throughout the year.

With an average temperature of 19°C (66°F) in July and a low of 5°C (41°F) in January, July is the hottest month in London, and

January is the coldest month. With 7, June has the most daily sunshine hours.

On average, winters in the United Kingdom will become significantly warmer; but cold or dry intervals will still occur. Summers in the United Kingdom are expected to become significantly warmer, but wetter summers are still possible. The UK has seen all ten of its warmest years since 2002. Climate warming has made heat waves like these summers in the United States 30 times more common. By 2050, heat waves like those plaguing the United States in 2018 are expected to happen every other year.

The summer maximum sunshine time in southern English coastal counties ranges from 294–420 hours in northern Scotland and Northern Ireland to 600–760 hours in southern England. Eastbourne had the most wonderful sunshine monthly in July 1911, with 383.9 hours.

According to the tourism score, the ideal season to travel to London for warm-weather activities is from mid-June through September. The tourism score prefers clear, rainless days with perceived temperatures between 65°F and 80°F.

The weather in the United Kingdom is sometimes unexpected, but it is rarely severe. Summer temperatures range from 9 to 18 degrees Celsius.

The average temperature is between 2 and 7 degrees Celsius in the winter, although temperatures regularly drop below 0 degrees Celsius. Thankfully, most homes, buildings, and buses have appropriate heat pumps.

Although this is due to the weather's unpredictable nature, the United Kingdom is commonly associated with rain. Rain doesn't just happen in one season; it can happen at any time of year and on any day. You could have magnificent sunshine, strong winds, and drizzle rain in one afternoon.

However, if you dress accordingly and have the right mindset, you can enjoy the UK rain or shine. Basking in the sun by the river, mud-dancing, or having a battle are all fun activities.

Although there is little variation across the UK's regions, northern and mountainous areas will have more snow, rain, and wind. The temperature in the United Kingdom is seldom intense, but it can change quickly. There could be warm sunshine, rain, and a chilly breeze on the same day. Bring a raincoat and multiple layers so you may add or remove them as the weather changes.

1.7 What should I bring for my travel to the UK?

Travelling light in the UK necessitates a certain degree of forethought and discipline, as all four seasons may be present during a visit.

The most acceptable packing advice for the UK can be summed up in one word: layers. Prepare to layer up and add on or pare down on a warm day, you can wear just a t-shirt, but if the weather drops, you can layer up with a jacket, a scarf, and a pair of tights for good measure. Keep in mind that you will require a coat regardless of the season - spring, summer, fall, or winter. The only variation is the weight and warmth of the garment concerning the season.

When travelling in the United Kingdom, the most important thing to remember is to be prepared for everything. The weather in the United Kingdom is infamous for being unreliable, and weather forecasts are no exception. So, you can expect cold, dark days even in the summer, while winter can bring unexpected sunlight and even a little warmth.

1.8 Prepare for border clearance

Given the excitement and discovery nature of the voyage, there is always a lot to pack; yet, before you can use the packed items, there is the hurdle of the country's border and embassy. So that your vacation and travel are not marred by confrontation and an overly harsh and inquiring attitude at the border. There are specific measures and actions that travellers must rigorously follow at the embassy for a smooth entry into the United Kingdom.

You'll need to show your identity document at border control, such as your passport or national identity card. To avoid delays, make sure your identification documents are readily available. If you're using a holder or wallet, take it out. If you're wearing sunglasses or a face mask, take them off. If you're travelling as a family, go through passport control jointly.

When you arrive at a port or airport in the United Kingdom, your identification document, such as your passport or identity card, will be scrutinized to confirm that you can enter the country in question. Your documents must be valid for the duration of your visit. In addition, you may need a visa to enter or transit the UK, depending on your nation.

Packing for your outdoor adventure is an essential part of the journey because these vacations allow you to appreciate how vast and lovely the world is, connect with nature, and put your worries behind.

Having the proper equipment also makes a huge difference.

It doesn't matter how much you pack or what your stuff costs. It's all about intelligent packing and knowing that you've taken the best first step toward having a good time. We'll assist you in packing appropriately to go adventuring in the United Kingdom like a pro.

1.9 Pack light but wisely
Packing light would make your trip much easier, but it will also save you money. Because many airlines are modifying their baggage size restrictions, choosing the proper backpack can make a difference in avoiding unpleasant surprises at the airport.

Because the last thing you want to worry about is a tear in your bag or a torn zipper lining, it's critical to invest in a high-quality technical backpack that can withstand the rigours of the aeroplane and outdoor travel. These bags are available in litre sizes so that you may choose the right one for the duration of your journey. If your trip exceeds more than a few days, you'll need at least a 55-litre container.

The weight of your luggage is also crucial, as you don't want to carry more luggage than you need. Consider how many days you'll be away from home, what's necessary for the trip, and what's just nice to have. Before packing everything, ask yourself at least once, "Do I need this on my trip?"

Focus on functional products for the vacation rather than non-essential fashion. If you are hiking for more than 5 hours a day, you'll need a pair of waterproof solid hiking boots and another pair of shoes or sandals that you can quickly put on and take off when it's time to relax in the evening. If the region is notorious for rain, you'll need moisture-wicking base layers like t-shirts and underwear that dry fast, a warm sweater made of a breathable fabric like merino wool, a packable raincoat, and thick socks with sock liners.

When visiting the United Kingdom, it's all about you and nature, so goods like makeup will take up valuable room. Accessories such as a hat and sunscreen will be far more helpful than the perfume or favourite clothing.

When you're ready to load your bag, put heavy goods at the bottom and separate pockets for an emergency kit, electrical devices, and other vital items you need to access quickly. Every day, separate your dirty and clean clothes and pack the filthy ones to the bottom of your suitcase. As you may have heard, rolling your clothes rather than folding them saves space and helps keep your bag more organized.

1.10 Bring a comfortable backpack with you

Aside from the apparent practicality of commuting, the modest backpack is an essential accessory if you want to be considered seriously in the United Kingdom. Not just any bag will do; it must fit comfortably over a coat, be sleek and non-lumpy, accommodate a variety of communication necessities, and provide easy access to train passes and other travel items. Strategic pouches and pockets in your bag or backpack are essential for panic-free travel. You'll know where your credit card, passport, wallet, and other valuables are at all times, and you'll avoid those awful moments of panic while scrambling through your belongings trying to find whatever is hidden beneath the last month's worth of receipts. So, with your sneakers on and your rucksack slung over your shoulder, you're finally looking like a mission-oriented local.

1.11 Weather-proof clothes

The key to packing clothing for a trip to the United Kingdom at any time of year is to carry a variety of layers that you can layer to adjust to the weather.

Warm clothing is the essential item to bring on your winter tour of the United Kingdom. Because the average winter temperature ranges from 0 to 7°C, you'll need to plan ahead of time how you'll dress for your vacation. Layering with pants, long-sleeved shirts, woollen sweaters or down jackets, and a water- and wind-resistant winter coat over the top is recommended.

People in cities in the United Kingdom are well dressed, so bring your nicer clothes, though you won't need to be overdressed for most events. However, if your travel plans include fine eating, excellent pubs, or visits to plays such as the opera or the West End, you may wish to dress up.

When visiting London in the winter, it is best to dress in jeans or pants. Layers with a warm sweater on top are an option. Winter essentials in London include a warm winter coat, a warm scarf, and excellent gloves.

There are a variety of glove brands available in the market. There are gloves with a toasty merino wool lining and magnetic finger covers specifically for photography. These are ideal if you expect to capture many photos while simultaneously protecting your hands from the elements.

Temperatures in the UK range from 17°C to 25°C in the summer, but don't be surprised if they surge much higher, prompting newspapers to declare a heat wave. Summers in London, in particular, may be scorching, so bring shorts, t-shirts, skirts, and dresses. Warmer layers, such as a waterproof coat, cardigans, and pants, should be packed because you never know when the weather will change. If you're prone to the cold, you can even wear thermals as your first layer. Remember that catching the tube in London or visiting shopping malls may get quite hot, so dress in layers that you can readily remove if necessary. Although visitors discover that jeans are uncomfortable to walk in on the occasional hot day, it is better to bring light pants or shorts. You'll also want a pair of sunglasses for bright days.

1.12 Shoes

When it comes to baggage space, shoes are always the killer, so wear your chunkiest boots on the flight and keep the lighter stuff in the suitcase. Travel shoes must always include some suitable, comfy footwear; nevertheless, you don't want to appear overly sensible. Spending time in any UK city, particularly as a guest, will entail some walking. Instead of using the tube everywhere, try to do as much as possible above ground in London. Take a moment to observe the architecture along your trip by looking up at the skyline. When you look beyond the tube map, the distances are often minimal, and it gives you a much greater sense of the city and where you are. Walking also gives you a better chance of finding that great coffee shop or that interesting tiny bookshop that you wouldn't see if you were sitting on a train underground. You can utilize the Citymapper app, which shows you where you can walk, take the bus, or take the train. Stay in a centrally located home, and you'll be in the perfect spot for exploring.

Frequent excursions break time spent in the Great Outdoors to pubs and other gastro restaurants in the UK countryside is more relaxed and informal than in cities. Again, layering is the best approach to well-prepared and well-packed. Suppose you get caught in a week of rain, head to any village's High Street, and pick up an excellent pair of wellies. It's perfectly okay to walk into a rustic restaurant or tavern wearing some practical wellies and a waterproof coat.

A good pair of shoes can mar or make your vacation. For example, as you visit the UK and its cities, you'll be doing much walking, and the last thing you would want is hurting your feet or blisters.

1.13 Electronics and smartphones

You can't deny the utility of a smartphone while travelling, regardless of your viewpoint. It doesn't have to be limited to sharing photos on social media. A smartphone combines a notepad, alarm clock, lamp, camera, phone, and offline map. It will not only serve as the most reliable backup in the event of an emergency, but it will also save you space.

A smartphone with a flat battery is useless. As a result, put a power bank at the top of your packing list. It will charge your camera, iPad, and other gadgets you like to travel with and maintain your smartphone's battery life green.

Because London is such a picturesque city, you'll want to carry some form of photography equipment with you on your trip. It doesn't matter if it's only a smartphone. If you want to take the most outstanding pictures, we recommend purchasing a dedicated camera and a tripod. It will also help you take better images with a selfie stick. When travelling with your camera, don't forget to bring a few extras; spare batteries, memory cards, a UV filter for the lens, and a good bag or case to keep everything secure are all critical. If you want to save extra money for a separate camera bag, a camera insert for your daypack or carry-on is good.

Remember that not all of your equipment will function if you travel to England from the United States, which utilizes a 110v system. Most laptops, phones, and cameras will work perfectly, but many hair dryers, curling irons, and straighteners, in our experience, do not support dual voltages.

1.14 Additional requirements

You'll want to pack your toiletries for your trip to the United Kingdom. You won't need anything special for the UK than you would for anywhere else, so bring your essentials: toothbrush, toothpaste, deodorant, moisturizer, and any makeup or sanitary goods you might require.

Of course, all of these items are readily accessible in the UK, but because brands may differ slightly, it is best to carry a product from home with you, to be specific. If you're on medications, make sure to bring them with you.

We also recommend sunscreen for summer travel and a decent moisturising lip balm for winter travel because the chilly winter air may quickly dry out your lips, which isn't nice.

Last but not least, let's get back to that luggage and our final must-pack item for your UK vacation. It will rain sometimes, so bring your umbrella unless you want to arrive at that posh restaurant or tour the Hampton Court Flower Show looking drenched.

CHAPTER 2: THE ULTIMATE EXPERIENCE GUIDE IN THE UK

One of the most enjoyable aspects of a UK holiday is the simplicity needed to explore the exciting and adventurous country. Because of its size, you may stay in cities like London or Liverpool and travel around the country by train, bus, or boat.

Although the United Kingdom is a small country, it is packed with more history, culture, and scenery than you can imagine. Big Ben, Buckingham Palace, and the Houses of Parliament are among the country's most recognized attractions, but it's much more than simply history and buildings. The city of London exudes metropolitan sophistication and attitude. There are examples of current trends and innovations all over the place. Eat-in chic restaurants, view cutting-edge architecture (the Shard) and broaden your cultural horizons with the city's vibrant cultural environment. Beyond London, you'll find the ancient rubbing shoulders with the modern.

Travel back to centuries-old cities like Oxford and Bath and picturesque villages and visit regal palaces and medieval cathedrals in England. On the other hand, northern cities such as Liverpool and Manchester wow you with their up-to-date vibes and personality.

There's also the scenery to consider. Inhale as you wonder at Scotland's beautiful highlands and lochs, the Giant's Causeway in Northern Ireland, and the sublime Welsh landscape and shoreline. The hospitality of the United Kingdom adds to the country's diversity. The decision is yours:
- Lodge in one of the world's most opulent hotels.
- Be hip in a boutique hotel.
- Cuddle in a quaint cottage or B&B.

While travelling to the United Kingdom without visiting London is possible, it is not recommended. The country's expansive capital has plenty of things to keep you entertained and exquisite resorts and hotels to keep you comfortable. Stonehenge, one of the The country's most known monument is a 90-minute train ride from the nation's capital. A one-hour train ride will get you into the heart of either Edinburgh or Glasgow.

The Tower of London is the best thing to do in London if you want to learn more about the UK's rich heritage. On the banks of the Thames, the historic 1,000year-old White Tower and the Jewel House, which houses the Crown Jewels, are located alongside the spectacular Tower Bridge.

Buckingham Palace, London's Royal residence, is a must-see for British Royal Family fans.

Buckingham Palace

Another must-see place in the UK is the city's Whitehall Road district, including the Parliament Buildings and Westminster Abbey, where numerous royal weddings occur.

South Kensington is another neighbourhood to visit in London. It houses some top institutions of the city, the Natural History Museum and the Victoria and Albert Museum. You must see the History Museum and the famed Harrods department store for the whole experience; visit Trafalgar Square, home to the National Portrait Gallery and the renowned Nelson's Column.

Explore 1000 years of history at London's castle, a secure fortress, royal residence, and infamous prison.

Prepare to be awestruck by the beautiful, internationally renowned Crown Jewels. Take a Yeoman Warder tour to hear gripping tales of anguish and passion, betrayal and torture. Discover why the ravens are famous as the Tower's guardians, and marvel at the majestic White Tower, a superb example of Normal architecture at the heart of the Tower of London.

The lodging location and your choice of hotels, inns, and settlements are critical parts of the journey if you want to experience and enjoy the best of the UK and all of its lovely qualities. The United Kingdom boasts an endless supply of hotels, guest homes, inns, and other accommodations with adventurous elements to satisfy guests and explorers. This list consists of places to visit in your settlement region and things to do and see.

2.1 The District of the Lake

The tranquil Lake District is the UK's largest and most visited national park, with majestic peaks and glorious lakes that have inspired many a poet. Windermere, England's longest lake, is still plied by vintage boats, and it was a favourite of Wordsworth's.

The town has a Beatrix Potter Museum, and a choice of luxury Lake District hotels is connected to a site near Sawrey where Miss Potter formerly lived by a cable-operated auto ferry. Ambleside, home of the Stock Ghyll Force waterfall, is located at the lake's northern tip.

A route leads north to Keswick, passing through scenic Grasmere and Thirlmere Lake. This lovely town is set by Derwent Water and is overshadowed by Skiddaw, with Scafell Pike, England's highest mountain, to its southwest. Bassenthwaite Lake is to the north, while Glen ridding is to the east, on the banks of Ullswater, a popular sailing spot guarded by Helvellyn.

2.1.1 Lake District

Coniston is a small community near a lake in the Southern Lakes that offers water sports. Barrow-in-Furness, a port town in the southwest, and Grange-over-Sands, with its long promenade, are on the sea. Kendal is noted for its delicious mint cake and boasts a museum dedicated to Lakeland life and several Lake District hotels with swimming pools.

Since poet William Wordsworth roamed here, the captivating icy-ground landscapes of Coniston have made it a magnet for lovers of the outdoors (lonely as a cloud). The Lake District, the UK's most visited national park, will attract even more admirers of its natural beauty, picturesque villages, cultural history, great outdoor activities, and distinctive gastronomy this year, thanks to its recent UNESCO listing.

You can still escape the crowds on the fell tops, but you can also relax and heal your hurting muscles in a boutique spa. Style and quality rise in the region's hotels, with some remarkable new debuts. The most beautiful of these are unquestionably Forest Side and Sharrow Bay, and the Gilpin, to name a few.

The new Forest Side hotel is all about sophistication, just as William Wordsworth came to Grasmere for a simple life. You can still tramp into the fells from here, but the new Forest Side hotel is all about simplicity. A gothic manor home has been renovated into delicately lovely, eco-friendly lodgings inspired by all things Lake District: even the Herdwick wool rugs were woven locally.

The Michelin-starred restaurant not only uses Cumbrian foods but also produces pickles and forages them before concocting spectacular tasting menus with them. So, when we claim the food here tastes like nothing else, we mean it. They are dog friendly and have beautiful furnishings, a terrific location, and delicious food.

The Lake District boasts breathtaking landscapes, rolling hills, and massive quantities of water, which will pique your attention. Sure, those are the main attractions, but there are plenty of other things to do between hiking, riding, and sightseeing.

In addition to plenty of mountainous terrains to explore, you'll find a plethora of fantastic eateries, watering holes, museums, and historic buildings. Beatrix Potter's former home, Wordsworth's old stamp shop, the country's last working mine, and gingerbread made according to a 160-year-old recipe is also part of its features. You can even break up all that fresh air with a night at the theatre.

Here is a list of the top adventurous things to do in the Lake District to have an ultimate adventure and experience, from Beatrix Potter's former house to England's highest peak.
Lake District Attractions.

2.1.2 Attend a performance at Theatre by The Lake;

The setting of this Cumbrian creative centre is one of the most beautiful of any theatre, with spectacular views of

Derwentwater that visit the café as enjoyable as watching something on the stage. It's highly worth acquiring a ticket for, as

this theatre is a highlight of any trip to the Lakes, thanks to its varied and always intriguing program.

2.1.3 Go on a hike to Castlerigg Stone Circle;

A remarkable and unusual collection of boulders dating from the Neolithic period was on par with Stonehenge. Walking to the circle from Keswick's town core takes around half an hour.

While you're there, watch out for grazing sheep that roam freely about the stone circle; this is a beautiful place to go if you're looking for something free and family or dog-friendly. The Stone Circle is aligned with the sun, so come for the summer solstice. It's one of the most peaceful midsummer festivities.

2.1.4 Visit the Windermere Lake;

This massive body of water is England's largest natural lake and an excellent example of the scenic Lake District. With its spectacular views and plethora of entertaining activities, Lake Windermere is a must-see on any vacation to the Lake District. You can walk, climb, cycle, or even Segway around it, but the water is where the most incredible fun is experienced. Get away from

the crowds and rent a car or a rowboat.

Don't worry, and you'll receive all the necessary training and safety instructions.

2.1.5 Visit The Lakes Distillery for a drink

A top-notch distillery that uses many local ingredients to make gin, whisky, and vodka. The Lakes Distillery is a relative newcomer to the market, debuting in 2014, but it's quickly establishing itself as a must-see in Cumbria. Tours and tastings are available every day, and on weekends, you may meet the alpacas who live there! If you wish to take something home with you, there's also a fully stocked shop.

There's also a tiny, friendly eatery nearby.

2.2 Netherwood Hotel

The Netherwood Hotel, a historic noble estate within expansive, colourful gardens, offers dramatic views across Morecambe Bay. The restaurant has a daily changing menu of local produce, and there is also an on-site spa and fitness centre.

Netherwood is a short drive from the Lake District National Park, and magnificent treks in the surrounding woodland and countryside are available. After a scenic 10-minute walk, you'll arrive in Grange-over-Sands town centre.

Guests can use the on-site fitness centre for free while using the on-site spa for a fee. It is necessary to book your thermal journey and any treatments in advance. Each en suite room offers a flat-screen TV and a hairdryer and has a view of the woodlands, gardens, or Morecambe Bay. If needed, room service is also provided.

2.3 Nanny Brow

This top-notch B&B in Ambleside will appeal to devotees of the Arts & Crafts movement. The mansion, designed in 1904 by architect Francis Whitwell, has been lovingly renovated, and each bedroom is uniquely adorned. The rooms have antique furnishings and modern bathrooms, and several have spectacular views. There's also a bar, and visitors can take a lounge with board games, long and short walks from the house (set in a six-acre garden), and guided hikes can be pre-booked; this is a mansion, a five-star, award-winning bed and breakfast in a superb Lake District location, to be exact. It's everything you'd imagine a phrase like this to be.

This colourful hotel lies in the centre of thriving Ambleside in more ways than one. First, there's the location: you can go out onto the main shopping street or up the track to knobbly Wansfell Pike, also visible from the spa. Second, it's a local institution, deeply rooted in the community and famed for having the town's brightest Christmas lights. The hotel provides reasonable mid-range pricing and has some high-end suites, evidenced by its high-standard public rooms, restaurant, and staff. It's housed in a lovely 17th-century structure, yet it's equipped with everything you'd need for a nourishing and pleasant stay in the twenty-first century and possibly beyond! Top walks are also right on the doorstep, so you can't go wrong.

2.4 The Inn of the Commodore

The Commodore Inn has a restaurant and is located in Grange Over Sands. Windermere is only 24 kilometres away, and Bowness-on-Windermere is about 23 kilometres. Leeds Bradford International Airport is 113 kilometres from The Commodore Inn.

Wireless Internet access is provided in public areas and is free of charge. Food and beverage, wine and champagne, kid meals, special diet menus, bar, restaurant, and daily housekeeping are part of the amenities and services available at the inn to ensure that guests have the best possible experience.

2.5 Inn Kirkstile

This secluded and ancient inn in the calmer western Lakes has nothing spectacular, fantastic hospitality, fantastic cuisine, excellent real ales, and great walking: Between Loweswater and Crummock Water, Kirkstile Inn is nestled against Melbreak crag.

The food is traditional pub fare with modern smarts, impeccably sourced and cooked, with no foam insight. The bedrooms are charming, and the food is standard pub fare with modern smarts, impeccably sourced and cooked, with no foam in the picture. There's an entire menu dedicated to sausages.

2.6 Manchester Hotel in Brooklyn

Stock Exchange Hotel is located in Manchester, 100 meters from the Royal Exchange Theatre, with a restaurant, private parking, a bar, and a communal lounging centre. The Manchester hotel has a bar, a shared lounge, and city views. Canal Street is 400 meters away.

In the centre of Manchester, a hip new hotel by Melia Newcastle is located in Newcastle upon Tyne, 700 meters from Sage Gateshead. It features a restaurant, a fitness centre, and a bar.

2.7 Interesting outdoor activities and places in the UK

A trip to the United Kingdom isn't just about visiting the best and most beautiful hotels and inns in the country and staying in the property and attractions that a guest house has to offer.

Although the UK is small, its scenery is vast and diverse, ranging from rolling green hills and ancient woods to magnificent mountain peaks, picturesque lakes, and rough moors. Take a journey of the UK's 15 National Parks to see all of the country's diverse landscapes.

The Lake District is known for its breathtaking landscapes, rolling hills, and massive water. Sure, those are the main attractions, but there are plenty of other things to do between hiking, riding, and sightseeing. You can even break up all that fresh air with a night at the theatre.

2.7.1 Climb Scafell Pike

With an elevation of 978 meters, Scafell Pike is the highest point in the United Kingdom. A trip to the summit and back will almost certainly leave you with blisters and skin that the wind or rain has blasted. But you'll also get a spectacular view of the National Park and a tremendous sense of accomplishment. Just be sure you've done your homework; this necessitates reviewing the mountain forecast and acquiring the appropriate equipment (primarily decent footwear). Sure, it's entertaining, but it's also a significant project.

2.7.2 Visit England's last functioning mine

Honister Slate Mine is England's last active mine and the source of green slate produced from Fleetwith Pike. This intriguing location offers a variety of activities for people of all ages and abilities. There's plenty to keep you occupied here, from a reasonably moderate excursion via subterranean mine shafts to mounting the side and inside of a mountain and traversing a terrifying infinity bridge. Honister is also home to the highest café in the National Park, which is nice. Make a beeline for a surprisingly decent souvenir shop, which sells items a step up from the usual pricey knickknacks.

2.7.3 Visit Hill Top and follow the Beatrix Potter route

The old house of children's author Beatrix Potter is lush and delightful, which she left after her death in 1943, together with thousands of objects and personal possessions, to the National Trust. You'll find furniture, pictures, odd China, Potter paintings, and much more at Hill Top and the opportunity to wander through her famed garden. If the Potter bug has bitten you, the National Trust has a downloadable 'Beatrix Potter trail,' which takes visitors around the Lake District locations that inspired her work.

2.7.4 Pay a visit to the quirky Derwent Pencil Museum

A strange but great museum about one of life's most banal aspects: the world's first pencil is housed in this small building, which sits in the shadow of the old Cumberland Pencils plant. There are also World War II spy pencils, an 8m coloured pencil, a café, and a shop. The 'Artist in Residence' courses, which feature prominent and local artists conducting classy-looking classes, are worth a look for aspiring painters.

2.7.5 Make yourself at home at The Mortal Man

From the low, panelled ceilings to the crackling log fire, this old-school inn and accommodations have oozed charm since 1689. Troutbeck Valley, home of The Mortal Man, is located just outside Windermere and Ambleside. The menu features typical British cooking that is especially delightful in the garden on a hot summer day. Keep an eye on the events calendar: depending on which nights you visit, you can enjoy live music, spoken word (performers receive a free drink), or quiz participation.

2.7.6 Overindulge in Grasmere Gingerbread

The sweet, ginger-flavoured dessert was born in this tiny boutique that sells the famed Grasmere Gingerbread. Sarah Nelson, a Victorian baker who had lived in the home, invented the recipe there in 1854. Since then, this delicately spiced, deliciously chewy gingerbread has been a great seller, and it's only available in a few places. Naturally, we recommend the shop or the Wordsworth Hotel next door, where you can sit and enjoy your gingerbread with a cup of tea. Try it with cheese, preferably from the Keswick Cheese Deli, one of the best in the Lake District.

2.7.7 Visit the Jurassic Coast and go fossil hunting

Located 95 miles south of London, the Jurassic Coast is noted for its unusual geology and England's longest coastline stretch. From Devon's Exmouth to Dorset's Studland Bay, the rocks document 185 million years of Earth's history and are also rather lovely. The beautiful cliffs of Beer and the medieval seaside resort of Lyme Regis are among the highlights.

- The arching shingle crest of Chesil Beach.
- The Rocks of Old Harry
- The golden sands of West Bay.

Not to be missed are Lulworth Cove, a beautifully blue remote beach, and Durdle Door, a majestic natural limestone arch.

2.7.8 Pay a visit to the Hawaii Volcanoes National Park

Kilauea and Mauna Loa, two of the world's most active volcanoes and countless historical and cultural treasures make this park the crown jewel of the Big Island.

From sea level to Mauna Loa's peak at 13,667 feet, this park is designated an International Conservation Area and an Archaeological Site. Before entering Thurston Lava Tube, take the following steps:

- Visit the Visitor's Center.
- See and feel the heat of steam vents.
- Observe Kilauea and Kilauea Iki craters.

2.7.9 Get a vantage point from Arthur's Seat

Edinburgh is one of the few cities that can claim to be home to an old volcano. Arthur's Seat, a grassy, craggy summit 351 meters above sea level, can be seen practically anywhere in the city and is only a short walk from the Royal Mile. To begin your ascent, go to Holyrood Park. Even though it's a short hike, it'll get your heart racing. Take a break at the summit and take in the views of Edinburgh Castle, the Scott Monument, and the surrounding area.

2.7.10 Take a tour of a premium Kona coffee farm

Take a cruise through the ancient Kona area in the heart of the coffee country. Inhale the mountain air while enjoying a wide range of Kona coffees from one of our favourite coffee roasters. Overlooking the vast Kona coastline, enjoy a delicious island-style continental breakfast. Overlooking the extensive Kona coastline, enjoy a delightful island-style continental breakfast.

2.7.11 Rainbow Falls

This 80-foot waterfall cascades into the Wailuku River below, passing through a natural lava cave. The Hawaiian goddess Hina, the mother of the legendary demigod Maui, is thought to reside in the lava cave beyond Rainbow Falls. Rainbows appear during the falls on a sunny day, creating a lovely scene.

2.7.12 Take a road trip.

Finally, if you are only allowed to do one thing outside, even if you don't perform any other outdoor activities, Have fun on the ride. The journey is as enjoyable as the goal on this road trip. You have the flexibility to stop and pull over whenever you choose. So, buckle in, turn up the music, and take in the stunning seaside vistas.

2.8 Itineraries to make the most of your time in the UK

Though travelling in the United Kingdom is quite simple, there are several logistical issues to consider to enjoy your vacation. The time of year you visit and the form of transportation you use to move about can impact your vacation. Even if you have set dates for your trip, it is still necessary to be aware of the potential weather conditions during your time in this country.

The weather in the United Kingdom varies drastically depending on where you go. Scotland will be significantly more fabulous in the winter than London. At any time of year, the further north you drive, the cooler it becomes. However, some seasons are better than others for visiting this beautiful part of the world, which is crucial to consider when planning a vacation to England, Ireland, or Scotland.

While getting ready for a trip to Great Britain, keep the weather in mind. There are four different seasons in the United Kingdom:

- March, April, and May are the months of spring.
- The summer months are usually from June through to August
- The Autumn season lasts from September through November.
- winter falls between December, January, and February

There are pros and cons to going throughout any season, but keep in mind that rain is always possible. With over 156 days of rain every year in the UK, an umbrella should always be on your packing list.

Seasonal changes have an impact on your vacation plans.

Summer is the most popular period to travel between London, Scotland, and Ireland. There are long days and days, and the weather is as comfortable as it gets. Summer highs in most of England and Ireland average around 20-22°C (68-72°F), whereas highs in Scotland are approximately 15-17°C (59-63°F). Though there will be wet days, you can expect more sunshine at this time of year than at other times.

Summer is not only beautiful (for Britain), but it is also the busiest season for tourists. The most beautiful cities and villages will be packed, and lodging will sell out months in advance. Prices will very certainly rise as well. If you're planning a trip to Edinburgh as part of your England-Scotland-Ireland itinerary, avoid visiting around August, when the city's world-famous Fringe Festival occurs. Accommodation sells out months in advance, and it may be extremely crowded.

Summer is the most popular tourism season in the United Kingdom, attracting international visitors and domestic vacationers. In England, schools close for six weeks in July, and students return to class in the first week of September. The most significant benefit of going in the summer is that the days are longer (with more daylight hours), and the weather is generally warmer. June is the sunniest month in the UK on average. You can plan to do and see more in the summer and take advantage of the lovely beer gardens adjacent to several pubs. While the weather in the UK can be warm to scorching throughout the summer, it is prudent to check the forecast, dress in layers, and bring an umbrella.

Autumn is undoubtedly the adequate time to visit the United Kingdom and Ireland because fewer tourists and pleasant weather are there. Autumn is the best season to tour the British Isles since it doesn't get too cold till November, so if you don't mind a little rain and need to wear a jacket, this season is the perfect time to visit.

Along with the stunning colours of the changing leaves, average highs in England and Ireland range from 10 to 17 degrees Celsius (50 to 63 degrees Fahrenheit) and between 8°C to 14°C (46°F to 57°F) in Scotland. Travel in late September or early October. You may be able to enjoy some glorious sunny days with temperatures above 20°C, and this is a popular season to visit the

UK because of the beautiful autumn foliage, traditional English events such as Guy Fawkes, and the pleasant weather. It's also would be quieter because the school would have resumed.

Spring in the United Kingdom and Ireland can still be reasonably chilly, as the weather doesn't begin to warm up until mid-to-late May, and it doesn't stay consistently warm until June. It can be rainy, windy, and miserable throughout most of the spring, and it can even be a little depressing because the leaves don't return to the trees until May. In the spring, highs in England and Ireland will range from 9°C to 14°C (48°F to 57°F), while in Scotland, highs will range from 7 to 13 degrees Celsius (45 to 55 degrees Fahrenheit). Spring presents an ideal time to visit the UK if you enjoy daffodils, bluebells, and the sight of lambs frolicking in a field.

THE BEST SPRING LONDON ITINERARY

Winter in the United Kingdom is marked by shorter days and lower temperatures (between 1 and 8 degrees Celsius). However, a chilly, crisp day with blue skies is always possible if the rain stays off. These days in London are ideal for sightseeing.

In Winter in the United Kingdom, days are shorter, giving less time for sightseeing, especially if you visit rural locations. With beautiful decorations gracing the streets, hot chestnuts for sale on street corners, and Christmas markets, London is also a lovely place to visit during the holiday season.

Also, keep in mind that temperatures drop a few degrees as you move north, so be prepared to fall in temperature whether you're visiting Scotland, Wales, Northern Ireland, or Northern England. Summer temperatures in the United Kingdom range from 14° C to over 21° C, with warmer averages in the southeast (i.e., London) and lower standards in Scotland. According to the UK Met Office, some country regions are wetter than others, with the north-west (particularly the Lake District), western and central Wales, and southwest England being the wettest.

Midges can be an issue in Scotland throughout the summer, so bring insect repellent if you plan on visiting during this period.

2.9 The finest spots to visit in the United Kingdom

The most challenging decision you'll make on your UK vacation will be deciding where to spend your time, determined by the length of your trip and your specific interests and priorities. Depending on the size of your travel and the vicinity to your destination. It's best to pick a few primary goals and build your schedule around them. You must carefully organize your visit.

Here are a few suggested itineraries on the top cities in the UK, as well as what to do to enjoy and have the best time in this modern but historic region for travellers who may only have limited time in the UK or who may have various travel interests:

• Visitors interested in English history should visit **Westminster Abbey** and **the Tower of London**. However, a stroll around Buckingham Palace would be a good opportunity to peek at one of the royals.

• Art enthusiasts can maximize their time at the Modern Tate and National Portrait Gallery, but theatre fans should purchase tickets to the Sam Wanamaker Playhouse. Admiring the structure and architectural view of **Tower Bridge** or the Cathedral of St. Paul's is another option: walking around one of London's many parks. In the evenings, guests can have fish & chips in a pub or sample the diverse dining options available in London.

• *Cardiff*, the capital of Wales, is a grossly underestimated city in the southwest of the United Kingdom. Take a train from London to Cardiff Central, where you'll learn your first words in Welsh; you have nothing to worry about, as everything is also in English. A day is enough time to explore the beautiful features of Cardiff, including Cardiff Castle, the National Museum, and Cardiff Bay. You can learn about Welsh rich historical heritage, traditions, and language by taking a walking tour and chatting with locals.

(National Museum of Wales)

• Early morning, cruise **Bristol**, take an interstate bus or train to Bristol, England, slightly east of Cardiff. On the west coast of England, Bristol is much smaller than London and does not possess as many tourist spots as other UK cities.

• Visit **Belfast**, Northern Ireland's capital, which has a complicated past with the rest of the UK and is not as well-known as places like London and Edinburgh. However, a tour of the United Kingdom would be incomplete without a stop here. Belfast Castle and City Hall are fantastic places to visit. Titanic Belfast is a must-see for anyone interested in the Titanic's history or fans of Leonardo DiCaprio's films. Spend the night here before flying to Edinburgh in the morning.

(Belfast street)

• Fly to **Edinburgh**, Scotland, to complete your journey. First, choose a hotel near the "Royal Mile," a stretch of Old Town that runs from Edinburgh Castle to Holyrood Palace. Then, climb the Seat of Arthur, drink in one of the city's historic bars favoured by the Scottish literati and see a few of the city's lesser museums and worship centres.

If you prefer to begin your journey in a more tranquil setting, you may start in Bath and end in London. You'll be more rested and prepared to take on Britain's most populous city. Bath and other destinations have direct bus connections from Heathrow Airport. Bath is also close to Bristol Airport. Settle in one of Britain's many enticing towns, such as York or Bath, for a slower pace of life. If villages call, stay in the Cotswold, where time seems to have stood still.

If you like major cities, you could easily spend a week in London, seeing world-class museums, sampling delectable cuisine, and taking in the sights and sounds of the city. Edinburgh and Glasgow are also exciting and lively cities to visit.

The *Lake District*, Wales, and the Scottish Highlands are fantastic places to visit if you enjoy nature. Pilgrimages to Stratford-upon-Avon (Shakespeare), Bath (Austen), and the Lake District (Austen) are famous among literary aficionados (Wordsworth and Potter). Golfers take a detour  to St. Andrews to tee off. Liverpool attracts Beatles lovers from all over the world.

2.10 The Best Way to Get Around

When it comes to organizing a journey to England, *Ireland*, and Scotland, many people believe that seeing a large chunk of each country by train is simple. While the railroad network is extensive, particularly in England, it can be costly, and it does not always link to smaller towns and rural areas.

In this London-Scotland-Ireland itinerary, we propose using the train and public transportation systems in England, then renting a car in Scotland and Ireland. Both countries are significantly more rural than England and lack a well-developed rail network.

Another option is to hop on the bus, which has more reliable connections within Ireland and Scotland than the train. Although bus tickets can be significantly less expensive than train tickets, it is usually cheaper to book tickets a few days ahead of time rather than on the day of travel.

Many locations on this ***Ireland and Scotland*** itinerary are significantly more accessible if you have transportation. Renting a car will help you access more off-the-beaten-path and difficult-to-reach places, allowing you to be more flexible. Nobody enjoys being at the mercy of erratic bus schedules.

If you plan to travel during this busy period, book your lodging, transportation, tours, and tickets as soon as possible.

CHAPTER 3: HELPFUL GUIDES TO THE UK'S

The country's beauty is partly from its diversified landscape and rich cultural past; beautiful historical estates and castles and world-class art museums and galleries are among the top sites to visit in the United Kingdom. Take in the culture of historic cities such as Edinburgh and Belfast and music meccas such as Manchester and Liverpool. Enjoy the fantastic wild terrains often described in the book and get active in the waters, whether surfing in the Gower or sailing in the Solent.

A 90-minute journey on the train from the nation's capital will get you to the lovely Salisbury; from there, a brief bus ride will get you to one of the United Kingdom's most renowned sites, Stonehenge. Finally, travelling between Edinburgh and Glasgow, an hour rail ride will transport you right into the city's heart.

3.1 UK's beautiful sights

The UK is full of adventure, from the hustle and bustle of London's streets to the calm of Snowdonia's valleys. Enjoy the frigid weather and stiff winds as you traverse the Scottish Highlands or the Lake District's mountains before relaxing with a craft ale next to a fireplace in a charming English village. However, one of the most enjoyable advantages of a getaway to the UK is how simple the simplicity of exploring the diverse and distinct features of the country is. Because of its vastness, you may settle down in cities like London or Liverpool and travel around the country by train, bus, or ferry to see the UK's beautiful sights.

3.1.1 London: The Ultimate Destination
While travelling to the United Kingdom without visiting London is possible, it is not recommended. The country's expansive capital has plenty of things to keep you entertained and exquisite resorts and hotels to keep you comfortable.

3.1.2 Edinburgh, Scotland's Capital

Edinburgh, the capital city of Scotland, is a well-known tourist destination in the UK. The magnificent Edinburgh Castle, ensconced in the city's several well-preserved medieval monuments, is the city's most famous landmark.

Every day, the legendary One O'clock Salute at Half Moonlight Point takes place at this 13th-century royal bastion located high above the ancient city on a rocky point. A visit to the National War Memorial of Scotland and the famous Stone of Destiny is a must-see. After 700 years in London, the British government recently returned the Stone of Destiny (the Stone of Scone) to Scotland.

Most of the city's other significant historical sites are within walking distance of the castle, such as the Royal Mile in the Old Town, home to stunning architecture and boutique stores, cafés, restaurants, and art exhibitions. The majestic historic Palace of Holyrood is also located here.

In addition to Edinburgh's Princes Street, which is a wonderful spot to shop and dine, the city's enchanting Royal Botanical Garden and Scotland's National Gallery are also worth visiting.

3.1.3 Roman-era Bath.

For almost 2,000 years, this charming city has enticed travellers to its therapeutic waters, which are called for its famous Roman Baths.

The water, which is thought to contain 43 minerals and has healing properties, runs at 275,000 gallons per day from three hot springs before spilling out at a steady temperature of 46.5 degrees Celsius. So while swimming in the historic Roman Baths is not feasible, visitors can enjoy the city's famous waters at several nearby spas, including the superb Thermae Bath Spa.

Bath is well-known and fascinating for its stunning Georgian architecture and historical significance. The most striking examples may be found along the beautiful, curved Royal Crescent, bordered by opulent town homes.

3.1.4 Stonehenge and Salisbury in the Middle Ages

Stonehenge has been a pilgrimage site for about 4,500 years, making it one of its greatest Historic Sites. Tourists visit to observe the incredible scale of this incredible testimony to humanity's ingenuity.

3.1.5 Windsor Castle

Windsor is a historic town conveniently positioned just west of London and provides a variety of tourist attractions. Among its many attractions are the magnificent Windsor Castle, the most well-known of the United Kingdom royal castles, which is situated along the banks of the River Thames and many antique half-timbered buildings along its charming old gravel alleys. This magnificent historic castle has been the summer residence of British nobles for almost a millennium.

3.1.6 Idyllic England the Cotswolds

With its 1,287 sq. km of magnificent terrain, the picturesque Cotswolds is arguably one of England's most photographed places. In addition, its unrivalled pastoral setting has earned it a reputation as one of the UK's most attractive destinations, with many people adding it to their bucket lists.

3.1.7 The picturesque Lake District

Cumbria's stunning Lake District is located near the Scottish border in the northeast of England. It is 1,448 square kilometres in size. Its unrivalled pastoral setting has earned it a reputation as one of the UK's most attractive destinations, with many people placing it on their bucket lists. However, because of its stunning surroundings, it is one of the most enchanting destinations to visit in the UK.

3.1.8 The Gower Peninsula

The Gower Peninsula, a lesser-known area of Wales, is a hidden gem waiting to be discovered. This location is an adventurer's dream, with some of the best surf surrounded by beautiful rolling dunes and hills. The Gower is a terrific spot to unwind and enjoy the peaceful and beautiful Welsh countryside, and it's not far from Swansea, a fast-growing seaside city.

3.2 What to eat in the UK

The United Kingdom has breathtaking scenery and some of the best cuisines in the country. As a result of the UK's unpredictable weather, the food represents what the British people want at the time: substantial, warm, and comfortable meals! These classic meals have become increasingly popular and are extensively eaten around the country, giving comfort eating a whole new meaning. Here are a few typical dishes to try if you want to get your hands on some of the best:

3.2.1 Fish and chips

The much-loved fish and chips are the most popular British dinner and a staple diet for a Friday night! You can find this delectable delicacy in nearly every pub, restaurant, and fish and chip shop, so don't leave without trying it with plenty of salt and vinegar.

3.2.2 Dinner with a Roast

The classic roast meal is a long-standing Sunday custom. On a Sunday, you'll find this dish, also known as Sunday Dinner or Sunday Roast, in every bar and restaurant for individuals who wish to go out for a big meal. You'll never forget your first, and it won't be your last, with a plate full of meat, vegetables, and potatoes piled high and drenched in gravy.

3.2.3 Breakfast with all the trimmings

Breakfast, too, begins with warmth and heartiness! Imagine your plate loaded high with greasy delights like sausages, eggs, beans, toast, hash browns, tomatoes, and more, wherever you are in the UK!

3.2.4 Pie with Steak and Ale

The hearty steak and ale pie is another British staple. This big dish is the gastronomic equivalent of a comfortable blanket and a crackling hearth, with a crispy and flaky shell filled with beef, cheese, and Guinness.

3.2.5 Chicken Tikka Masala

This creamy Indian dish, which is said to have originated in Glasgow, is usually flavourful and eaten with savoury rice and herby naan bread. It is available at every Indian restaurant and pub, and you can be sure it will be delicious!

3.2.6 Bangers and Mash

Nothing beats a stodgy supper like sausages and creamy mash to warm your insides and give you that contented grin! Even though it's one of the most straightforward dinners to prepare, you won't be disappointed with this dish, whether you order it at a bar or a friend's house. You'll almost certainly come back for more.

3.3 The best hotels and places to stay in the UK

In the United Kingdom, lodging can be pretty costly, especially if you book last minute. However, there will always be somewhere to stay, whether in the city or the countryside, thanks to couch surfing and camping worldwide and hostels, BnBs, hotels, and Airbnbs.

It's essential to reserve accommodations if you visit during the high season or around holidays. These are some of the most outstanding hotels and lodging options for visitors and tourists in the United Kingdom. Although the number of hotels and guest houses in the United Kingdom is endless, here are a few to get you started:

3.3.1 The Gainsborough Bath Spa England

On the inside, this stunning eighteenth-century Georgian building transforms into an equally stunning modern hotel, complete with naturally heated mineral water from Bath's renowned underground wells. Walking in seems like walking from the past into the future. But, on the other hand, a toga wouldn't look strange among the spa's columns and mosaics, which were influenced by the Romans who built Bath. The Gainsborough is a true luxury hotel, offering various spa services and fine dining options. Gainsborough's Georgian furniture is tastefully plain, allowing the lofty rafters and huge windows to scream for themselves. The guestrooms are decorated in relaxing turquoise and brownish, with plush mattresses and high-end cosmetics; however, book one of the three Bath Spa suites, including tubs with three plumbing fixtures: heated, chilled, and natural thermal water.

3.3.2 The Grand Hotel in Edinburgh

It's hard to believe that the Edinburgh Grand, a former hotel transformed into a bank and back again, has survived the renovation process. Nevertheless, something is striking about the bank's foyer, with its polished black-and-white marble floors and colourful raspberry-pink circular sofa and a stunning spiral stairway that makes for a fantastic Instagram shot once you climb to the top. In addition, Hawksmoor, Edinburgh's first luxury restaurant, has a fantastic outlet.

3.3.3 Hotel Foxhill Manor Private House

The Foxhill Manor, a five-bedroom, three-suite sister hotel to the nearby Dormy, mixes the conveniences of a full-service hotel with the casualness of home, including spots where you can serve yourself a drink or two from the library metal framed. Because of the superior rooms, celebrities such as U2 and Lady Gaga have covertly stayed at the hotel, housed in a stone structure built in 1909. Scandinavian design features include vintage leather swivel armchairs, orange semi-circular sofas, and opulent fur rugs, but the antique fires remain. Farm-to-table certified with a twist, Chef Curtis Stewart's menu features chicken liver parfait "ice cream cones" on brioche wafers. He'll prepare burgers with hand-cut fries if you reserve the viewing room. The next day, go for a walk down the valley to burn it off.

3.3.4 Cromlix

The purchase of this carefully renovated Victorian mansion on 34 hectares of Scottish forests by tennis player Andy Murray, who hails from this part of Perthshire, hit the headlines in 2014. Yet, despite his fondness for this part of the Highlands, there's little evidence of the pro here. Albert Roux heads up Chez Roux at Cromlix, a renowned French chef who provides exceptional French-Scottish food. There are also private dining rooms and a whisky room where visitors can relax or sample a choice of Scottish whiskey. But, as on every Scottish estate, it's all about daytime activities on this Scottish estate. Cromlix provides tennis instruction, loch fishing, archery, garden games, and falconry on its Wimbledon-grade courts.

3.3.5 Hotel Kimpton Clocktower

A new hotel in Manchester, the Kimpton Clocktower, has been dubbed "the best new hotel in the city in a decade." With glazed bricks, subway tiles, panelled walls, stained glass, and carved wooden staircases, this Grade II–listed building, which first opened as the Refugee Guarantee HQ in 1895, has been elegantly refurbished to retain its commercial beauty. Under the soaring dome of the lobby, a 1,300-pound copper stallion created by Charles' granddaughter Sophie Dickens looms over the braking distance once used for horse-and-cart deliveries. The 270 rooms and suites are divided into three structures, each distinct shape and design. Art Deco touches can be seen in numerous places throughout the house, including neutral walls, green velvet on the chaises and headboards in the bedrooms, graphic art prints, wire lampshades in the bathrooms, black and white tiling in the bathrooms, Royal bathtubs and sinks, and Elemis as well as Grand Vetivert soaps in the bathrooms.

3.4 Shopping in the UK guide

A vacation in the UK always necessitates shopping, and when visiting the United Kingdom, you must have a comprehensive list. This list includes the top shopping destinations, from high-end couture to local street markets.

The UK enjoys global supremacy in terms of export and import of apparel and accessories, food goods, paper, and other miscellaneous commodities, with its strong point being skilled trading with the rest of the globe. If it weren't for the art, the United Kingdom would have to be a shopper's paradise, given its proximity to the world's aesthetic capital, Europe. So, here's a quick rundown of the best shopping spots in the United Kingdom:

3.4.1 Gateshead Metro Centre

The shopping centre, also known as the "intuMetroCentre," is located in Dunston, on the Tyne River's southern bank, and spans over 22,00,000 square feet. The shopping and entertainment complex features high-end retail outlets and more than 50 food options. It also has a movie theatre and a bowling lane, making it a full-fledged family entertainment centre. The MetroCentre is the biggest shopping mall in Great Britain and Europe, with top-notch eateries and Platinum Mall's most famous designer brands.

3.4.2 Manchester's Trafford Centre

The Trafford Centre, just a few kilometres outside of Manchester City, is one of the country's largest and busiest shopping complexes. Aside from the various top-end retail businesses, the shopping mall also has a recreational unit consisting of a cinema, an underwater aquarium, and a Legoland in its peripheral, making it an ideal weekend destination for families.

3.4.3 Market on Portobello Road

It is London's most prominent street market, selling antiques and one-of-a-kind items. The Portobello Road Market in Notting Hill features everything from antique clothing to art and furniture. It's an ideal day out for individuals seeking variety, not just in terms of people but also in food and collectables. Except on Sundays, the market operates between 8:00 a.m. and 6:30 p.m. every day. Saturdays are busier with auctions, which may be overwhelming for some due to the large crowds. On the plus side, the flea market offers great deals on antique clothing and handicrafts. Visitors may find burgers, muffins, and beer in various cafes and restaurants throughout the market.

3.4.4 Bluewater Shopping Centre

The centre is one UK's most popular shopping destinations. Pirate Cove Adventure Park, Dinotropolis, Gravity Trampoline Park, and Sega Activity Zone are among the theme parks on the site. It also features various food alternatives, ranging from afternoon tea shops to multiple cuisines and confectioneries. It has an ice rink and hosts a variety of public activities.

3.4.5 Brick Lane Market

Shopping in London, United Kingdom, does not have to be limited to designer labels and high-end boutiques. This East London market has a wide range of food vendors and antique shops. Brick Lane Market excels at selling one-of-a-kind products, from vintage clothing to second-hand furniture. It's a colourful place to go through because it's full of street art. A wide variety of Bangladeshi and Indian goods, such as vibrantly coloured textiles and spices, are accessible on the market.

3.4.6 Other Interesting areas
- Bury Market
- The Lakes Sculpture
- Carlton Centre
- The Lowry
- Watts Gallery (Watts Gallery)
- Artist's Village

3.5 A guide to historic sites and locations

From Roman dominance through medieval legends, civil wars, witches, and world wars, the United Kingdom's history is diverse. And, miraculously, we can see it through the magnificent castles, palaces, estates, and ruins that still survive today, each with intriguing stories to tell.

For travellers searching for a place to visit, here's a list of historic sites from around the UK that are wonderful for learning about different kinds of history. We hope they pique your interest, with everything from medieval castles, fortresses, and abbeys to cruel prisons, opulent royal mansions, and even a mystery witches museum.

3.5.1 North Cornwall's Museum of Witchcraft and Magic

This independent museum, hidden in the small Cornish village of Boscastle, houses a collection of remarkable witchcraft-related relics and explores the incredible role that magic and sorcery have played in British history.

3.5.2 Belfast, Northern Ireland, Titanic

To begin her infamously fateful voyage, a sailor built the Titanic ship in Belfast before sailing to Southampton on April 10th, 1912. Titanic Belfast, which launched in 2012, offers a fascinating look into the ship's history and a voyage through nine interactive galleries, attractions, and displays.

3.5.3 Buckinghamshire's Bletchley Park

Bletchley Park is a must-see for everyone interested in 20th-century history. Bletchley Park was Britain's premier decoding centre during WWII, housing the top-secret Government Code and Cypher School. Their work decoding enemy transmissions significantly impacted the war's conclusion, with analysts estimating it cut the fight by two years.

3.5.4 *Other historic sites and locations*
- Warwick Castle is located in the county of Warwickshire.
- Somerset's Roman Baths
- Isle of Wight's Osborne House

3.6 Nightlife in the United Kingdom

Another well-known feature of the United Kingdom is its nightlife. When visiting the United Kingdom, many tourists look for beautiful locations to enjoy the vibrant nightlife.

However, not all of our UK cities and towns have the same level of nightlife. Some areas offer many bars and pubs to pick from, while others are much quieter and have a smaller number of options.

When it comes to safety, British towns and cities vary considerably. While many of the top nightlife venues have plenty of staff and door supervisors, safety is still an essential element that many of us consider when arranging a night out in the town, so there is nothing to worry about in your nightlife search.

So, you're wondering which UK places are the finest for bars and pubs and safety? We can identify the most incredible spots for a night out and the top locations just for safety and drinking by looking at the UK's main towns and cities.

- Glasgow's Sub Club
- Smith House in England
- Tup Tup Palace
- Ocean View Room
- The Rainbow Locations
- The Full Moon Public House

They are a handful of the most popular nightlife destinations in the United Kingdom.

3.7 The best museums in Great Britain

3.7.1 Sir John Soane's Museum, London

Sir John Soane's Museum on England's Lincoln Fields is the world's first architectural museum. The museum had remained a public museum since Sir John Soane's death in the early 1800s when he gave it to the nation.

3.7.2 The British Museum in London

The British Museum, the first national public museum globally, is located in the heart of Bloomsbury. Sir Hans Sloane died in 1753, and the museum was founded following his death. He left his collection to King George II, who established the British Museum through an Act of Parliament. Sloane's collection was the first to be created. Over eight million artefacts from various cultures worldwide are now housed in the museum. The world-famous Rosetta Stone, acquired in 1802, and the Elgin Marbles, which they added to the collection in 1816, are two of our highlights.

3.7.3 Duxford, Cambridgeshire's Imperial War Museum

Founded in 1917, the Imperial war museum documents World War I events after Sir Alfred Mond recommended the establishment of a museum to commemorate all aspects of war. It is the first museum opened in London in 1920, while IWM Duxford opened in 1976 as a historical homage to aviation activities throughout World Wars I and II.

During World War I, the airbase at Duxford was created and served as one of the first Royal Air Force installations. It has played an essential role in British aviation history: in 1940, it was from Duxford that militants foiled Luftwaffe attacks on London. The museum is now brimming with history, providing visitors with an unforgettable experience. It is well-known as the European heartland of aviation.

3.7.4 National Railway Museum of Yorkshire

Yorkshire Museum is the largest train museum world. Today, the museum is separated into two locations, one in York and the other in Shildon. Various railway corporations have gathered railway antiquities since the late 1800s. Collections were brought together when the railways were nationalized in 1948, later utilized during the 1975 inauguration

ceremony of the National Railway Museum. The museum, built in a massive former steam locomotive depot, was the first national museum outside London. Its companion museum in Shildon, the first national museum erected in the northeast, opened in 2004. Queen Victoria's favourite carriage, which she referred to as her "castle on wheels," is displayed at the museum.

3.7.5 London's Royal Academy of Arts

A London art and artist institution. In 1768, Sir William Chambers petitioned King George III to form a club to encourage the arts and design. Before settling in 1867 at the Palladian Burlington House, the society visited various properties. The academy's primary concentration is British art, with exhibits ranging from the 18th century. The independent art institution conducts the Summer Exhibition every year, the most popular yearly  event in the last two centuries. It houses works by British masters like Constable and Hockney.

3.7.6 Scotland National Museum, Edinburgh

The National Museum was founded in 1985 in its current form to tell Scotland's story. The Royal Scottish Museum and the National Museum of Ancient artefacts combined to form the National Museum of Antiquities and the Royal Scottish Museum. When it was opened, it was the Scottish's largest multi-disciplinary museum. The collections were given to the Society of Antiquaries of Scotland by David Steuart Erskine, 11th Baron of Aberdeen, who formed the society in 1780. The structure was renovated in 2011 after a £47.7 million refurbishment, garnering them an architectural award for 'Best Building.'

3.7.7 Oxford's Pitt Rivers Museum

3.7.8 Liverpool Tate Modern

3.8 THE BEST CASTLES IN GREAT BRITAIN

In the British countryside, hundreds of castles stand guard as reminders of the technological prowess of previous generations. These structures, including large fortresses overlooking the shore, previous strategic strongholds, and others still inhabited today, serve as a reminder of the island's turbulent history. In addition to learning about the country's history and traditions, you may take advantage of the country's beautiful outdoor spaces and rich early autumn landscape while visiting these majestic castles.

3.8.1 Windsor Castle

It is located just outside London. The castle was a royal home for about 950 years and is the world's oldest and largest castle, with many rooms. Windsor Castle is a popular weekend resort for the Queen and a venue for national events and royal weddings. The Round Tower, which rises atop the oldest part of the castle,

dominates the skyline. At the same time, St George's Chapel serves as the Organization of the Garter's spiritual abode, a chivalric order that dates back to Edward III's reign in 1348. visitors should reserve the castle in advance.

3.8.2 Warwick Castle

It is possible to get a glimpse of medieval life at Warwick Castle, a massive stronghold in the heart of the Midlands. Learn about the castle's 1,100-year history by passing beneath its majestic portcullis, walking along the ramparts, seeing archery demonstrations, and browsing

through 64 hectares of gorgeous lawns. The Horrible Histories Maze transports kids back through time, while the Castle Dungeon uses real actors and spine-tingling special effects to reveal some of Warwick's darkest secrets.

3.8.3 Highclere Castle

After four seasons on television and a feature film, Highclere Castle in Hampshire, one of the stars of Downton Abbey, was transformed into a movie set. Lord Barry Charles, the architect of London's Houses of Parliament, transformed Highclere in the mid-nineteenth century from a medieval manor. Gardens dating back to the 13th century and 1,000 acres of

beautiful parkland created by the renowned landscape designer Capability Brown are available for visitors, as are tours of the estate's numerous rooms, including those used as state chambers in the Downton Abbey television series. Since 1679, the Baron and Baroness of Carnarvon have resided in the castle. And it has a one-of-a-kind display of Egyptian artefacts commemorating the role of the fifth Baron of Carnarvon in the discovery of Tutankhamun's tomb.

3.8.4 Castle Bamburgh

Bamburgh Castle has a rich and intriguing history, sitting on a rocky ledge above the Northumberland Coast. It was originally built as an Anglo-Saxon fortress. The massive fortification was constructed early after the Norman invasion and has since served as a royal court for successive kings. Bamburgh Fortress, which was invaded during the Wars of the Roses, was the first stronghold to be attacked with explosives. A lovely collection of antiques and treasures reveal so much about the house's history.

Other notable castles include;
- The Stirling Castle
- Leeds Castle
- Dunrobin Castle

3.8.5 Castell Castle

3.8.6 Urquhart Castle

CHAPTER 4 TRIP PLANNING

4.1 practical tips for the best experience in the UK

Great Britain is a land rich in culture and natural beauty, and it is one of the world's most popular vacation destinations. Exploring this region of Europe can provide you with a pleasant time, whether you are looking for a peaceful or educational vacation. However, before embarking on any journey overseas, we recommend familiarizing yourself with the most necessary information. For each visitor or traveller to the United Kingdom, the following information is essential:

4.1.1 Currency:
The Pound Sterling is the official currency of the United Kingdom. If you intend on having any cash with you and don't have time to exchange it before your journey, there are several venues in the UK where you may do so.

4.1.2 Visa:
If you travel to the UK for holidays or short trips in less than six months, visas usually are not required; this applies to all EU, EEA and Swiss citizens. Most Asian and African citizens, on the other hand, will need to apply for a visa and will be limited to a 6-month stay in the country. Always double-check your country's visa requirements.

4.1.3 Electricity Socket:
There usually are three rectangular prongs on power outlets there.

4.1.4 UK Transportation:
You can take buses for as little as £5 for minor routes and £40 for more considerable distances. Train tickets range from £7 to £60 depending on the length, but they are fast, clean, and pleasant, and stations are located in every city.

4.2 Tips for having the best experience in the UK

This book contains essential UK TRAVEL TIPS to assist you in planning a vacation, including budgeting advice and things to see and do. Here are some fundamental practical guidelines for visiting the United Kingdom that you should know and put in place before embarking on an exciting adventure.

4.3 Tips on how to save money while touring Great Britain

The United Kingdom is not cheap to visit, so be aware of the approximate costs before departing. At first glance, London may appear to be one of those exorbitantly priced cities where your money vanishes. That, however, does not have to be the case.

Worst-case scenario: you run out of cash while on vacation. It'll be awful to return home after a fantastic trip only to learn that you've spent most of your money. So, plan ahead of time, develop a budget, and set a spending limit. When life throws you a curveball and you don't have a plan, it's tempting to become frivolous with your money. To avoid this, make a budget to set a spending limit as soon as possible.

Here are some suggestions and programs to help you manage your finances and save money.

4.3.1 Make a Reservation in Advance

Whether it's lodging, transportation, or sightseeing, we recommend making arrangements. Not only will you be getting on the bus or train, but you will also save a significant amount of money. The later you buy your tickets, the higher the price will be; this is especially true in the case of public transportation. When it comes to tourist attractions, many of them manage the flow of visitors, so you might not be able to purchase a ticket on the spot. If this isn't an unexpected vacation, make a schedule and book everything ahead of time.

4.3.2 Purchase before flying

You'll save money, and you'll be able to start filling your diary with exciting activities, such as a visit to Cardiff Castle or a tour through the Making of Harry Potter studio. What a wonderful experience.

4.3.3 Spend less money on transportation

For a couple of weeks, renting the smallest automobile with a manual transmission will cost £350-£500. When you factor in the price of gasoline, hiring a car in a country with great railways and public transportation may not be such a good option.

Other modes of transportation can help you save money. Take the tube in London, sample the rail system in the United Kingdom, and take the train. Purchase a British Rail pass for complete freedom. Taking the bus is even less expensive.

4.3.4 Save money by eating traditional English cuisine

Restaurant lunches range between £10 and £20 per person.

Any country's food is an integral part of its culture and legacy, and the United Kingdom has many dishes to boast on. Begin with an English breakfast, including sausages, eggs, bacon, beans, bread, and extra side dishes. Next, don't forget to taste Fish & Chips, which this cuisine can find at almost every local restaurant. Meat pies and roast meals are very popular among the English, it is also known as Sunday Dinner or Sunday Roast, and it consists of a plate of meat, mashed potatoes, and vegetables. All of these are covered in gravy; guests can find this in any bar or neighbourhood café, so give it a try to enjoy the complete experience!

4.3.5 See if you can catch a show

The United Kingdom is well-known for holding some of the world's most prestigious festivals; this includes music, folklore, light festivals, and various other activities! We strongly recommend seeing a show in addition to strolling around the cities, viewing the most prominent tourist attractions, and sampling the cuisine. The schedules for the coming year are usually available online, and you will undoubtedly discover some that interest you. Glastonbury, one of the world's most prominent music and performing arts festivals, takes place in the UK each summer, featuring top musicians from across the world and music genres such as rock, pop, techno, and many others.

4.3.6 Take a walk whenever possible

Many of the city's attractions are within walking distance of one another; walking between them could save you money on transportation. Start at Tower Bridge and stroll west along the river to see Tate Modern, trailing through the Coca-Cola London Eye and the Houses of Parliament.

You may look for a self-guided London walking tour to get an idea of a route that would allow you to view several of the city's most well-known landmarks. There are also free walking tours available to let you see and learn about some of the city's most famous sights. You might like to leave a small tip during these tours as a thank you.

4.3.7 Make use of a contactless card or an Oyster card

There are different ways to use public transportation in London if you require it; this includes purchasing a paper ticket from a station, using contactless (such as your bank card), or purchasing an Oyster Card. Then, once you've used your contactless card or Oyster for a specific period, your travel will be capped. Although this varies based on the zones, you're passing through and whether you're travelling during peak times.

4.3.8 Save money by sightseeing

Consider acquiring a heritage pass from the Wildlife Trust, English Heritage, or National Highland if you plan on visiting several of Britain's important cultural sites. Visitors with a token could save money when visiting hundreds of sites, like the ancient Stonehenge, instead of paying individual entry fees.

4.3.9 Free historical tours

Every September, thousands of old landmarks and structures, particularly those normally inaccessible to the community, offer their services for free! Heritage Open Days are held all around England, including well sites and lesser-known gems opening their doors. Heritage Open Days are held across the country, whereas Open House London focuses on the capital. Hundreds of properties in Northern Ireland take part in European Heritage Open Days, while Doors Open Days in Scotland allow visitors to see the sights. Wales welcomes visitors and will enable them to visit attractions such as medieval abbeys and radio museums.

4.3.10 Take use of low-cost internet sites

Register for Regular Table to access a special page with discounts at restaurants across the UK, including half-price deals. Subscribe to Groupon to access a variety of discount vouchers valid across the United Kingdom. There's under £100 a night of accommodation in stately homes and castles, 50% off luxury brunch experiences, and a few off-the-beaten-path options.

4.3.11 Take advantage of free attraction

Buckingham Palace, Tower Bridge, parks, and most museums are among the free attractions in London that are perfect for saving money. Several major museums, including the Natural History Museum, the Tate Modern, the British Museum, and others, are open to the public. If you are interested, many museums feature paid exhibitions that you can attend.

4.3.12 Keep an eye out for lunch specials

The competitiveness between businesses is a positive aspect of London, making room for many low-cost lunch options. For example, supermarket meal deals cost roughly £3 for a sandwich, snack, and drink. Restaurant lunch specials or quality and inexpensive takeaways are also options. Whatever your financial constraints, you should be able to discover something that meets your needs.

4.3.13 Stay in a hostel or Airbnb

If you stay in a middle-class hotel, you can expect to pay around £40 to £100 each night, but some cheaper options were only costing £15-35 per night if you're on a tighter budget. In 2020, the average cost of a night in a UK hotel will be just under £100. The average price of suitable hotel accommodation in most major cities still exceeds £100, with London and Edinburgh leading at almost £200. Take a look at some of these suggestions for saving money on lodging. If you're going to London, check out some of the cheaper locations to stay just outside the city; Airbnb and hostels are great options.

Airbnbs and hostels are beneficial for a variety of reasons. For starters, they are frequently located in desirable places. Second, compared to hotels, you can typically find considerably better deals, and they can also handle large groups. Finally, if you stay in an Airbnb or hostel, you will normally have access to kitchen facilities, allowing guests to prepare your meals rather than eat out. For these reasons, this lodging is ideal for folks travelling on a budget and wanting to save money.

Even though the most famous summits can receive hundreds of visitors each day during peak season, with some forethought, you can still enjoy even the most well-known mountains in relative tranquillity.

4.4 Tips for making the most of your time in London

Hiking, cycling, horseback riding, sailing, and more exciting sports like hang gliding, scuba diving, and spelunking are all available. The list of things to do and see in this beautiful country is endless, so if you don't plan, you'll find that time is rushing by before you've had a chance to see it all.

Trying to cram too much into your UK holiday could leave you exhausted and dissatisfied. However, as you are unlikely to cross an ocean regularly, you will want to make the most of your stay.

The UK has all the variety you'd expect from a country with rich and ancient history. Despite this, it's all crammed into a bit of area of land. With so much within close reach, it's easy to go insane trying to see and do everything. It's much better to design your trip around one or two activities that you truly enjoy.

So, how can you save time, get the most out of your experience, and make the most of your time?

4.4.1 Get up early or stay up late

A vital piece of advice is to visit the site during off-peak hours. Of course, this could entail ridiculously early beating the early birds or staying up late to avoid the evening rush. However, seeing the world's most stunning vistas at daybreak or as the stars come out can offer a truly intimate and breathtaking experience; you'll be glad you set your alarm, even though it can feel a little painful on your vacation – after all, you're supposed to be relaxing and resting.

Summertime sunshine may arrive painfully early, but getting out of bed at the crack of dawn or before is a sure-fire way to snag a few uncrowded hours on even the busiest hill. You may easily find yourself alone on the summit of Tryfan or Scafell Pike with the help of a loud alarm clock and a strong cup of coffee while the sluggish masses are still picking over their B&B sausages and beans.

The tail end of the day can be as empty as early dawn because most walkers seem to cram their activities into a few short hours. As tea time approaches, the hills become increasingly deserted, and if you can withstand the onslaught of humanity, you might soon find yourself high and dry on your private hilltop island. Although the crowds may have departed the peaks early in the evening, there may still be hours of acceptable light left in the day. Summer sunsets are late, which makes for excellent views and photographs. Why not stay a little longer? There's nothing to fear in the dark with a headlamp and a sense of adventure, and after dark, you can almost always count on having the place to yourself.

4.4.2 Make a reservation via the internet

This is a tip that never fails. If you go past a ticketed site, such as Madame Tussauds in London or the Louvre in Paris, you'll notice two lines: one for those who have pre-booked online or by phone, and another for those who are paying on the day. We don't need to tell you which one is ALWAYS the shortest. Booking online can save you HOURS of queuing time and money, so do it whenever you can.

4.4.3 Switch up your food patterns

Typical local dinner times, popular restaurants worldwide will always have a lengthier wait. If you run into theatregoers in New York or London, expect to wait well over an hour for lunch.

To counteract this, eat a little earlier or later than usual. Easy and quick access to The Devonshire Restaurant and its delectable menu will make battling crowds (and your hunger!) a breeze for visitors of The Devonshire.

4.4.4 Hire a personal guide

If you have the time and money, hiring your guide to take you on a (very much) access-all-areas tour around the site is a great opportunity to gain an insider's view of some of the world's most famous attractions.

They'll be able to tell you everything you need to know about the location and provide expert recommendations for other fun things to do around. These kinds of advisers for hire can also be surprisingly economical.

4.4.5 Seek advice from the locals

After all, they are the most familiar with your new surroundings. They'll have spent years visiting (or avoiding) the hotspots, so they'll know the optimum times and days. Start a conversation with a local at a pub or restaurant, or cab drivers are known for providing insider information. If you don't know anyone in the city, you can approach a server at the restaurant, who will gladly assist you.

4.5 How to beat the crowd in the UK

Large crowds are almost inescapable at some of the UK's most popular attractions. After all, no vacation to England is complete without a stop at the London Tower, and no journey to London is complete without a stop in the Lake District. And no trip to London would be complete without attempting to spy on the queen at Buckingham Palace.

So don't feel obligated to stay away from these locations. You simply need to be a little more strategic in your visit planning. Here are some tried and true techniques for avoiding crowds at popular attractions in the United Kingdom to get you started.

4.5.1 Act as a sleazy pit stop

What's better than an early start and a late end if you're looking for solitude? Spend the entire night up there is the apparent option. A masochistic novelty exists in a dusk-to-dawn shift on your feet, but sleeping out will achieve the same objective if your body clock baulks at such intense nocturnal wandering. You and the night-time mountain just be you if you camp or hive on a high ridge or in a secluded cove.

4.5.2 A meal and some local knowledge

Consider avoiding some of the busiest routes. Although you'll undoubtedly want to explore the main attractions in your new surroundings, you might want to bypass some of the major attractions in favour of seeing some of the more off-the-beaten-path delights. This is a fantastic way to avoid the crowds and explore the city like a local. Read blogs written by real locals in the region to learn about the finest places to visit.

4.5.3 Pay attention to the weather prediction

When the weather isn't so wonderful, especially in countries and places where heavy rains aren't usual, you're likely to find a lot more peace and quiet on the streets and at the major attractions.

Rain may be a powerful deterrent, with many people preferring to stay indoors rather than brave the storm. However, keep in mind that rain does not stop anyone or anything in some nations, such as the United Kingdom and France.

4.5.4 Travel during the off-season

It's a good idea to organize your entire trip around quieter seasons and visit sights at specific times of the day to avoid the busiest times. But, of course, this will change depending on where you're travelling, as different UK cities have different peak hours.

4.6 Top tips for selecting the best accommodation

Choosing where you will stay and stay throughout your tour of the United Kingdom is just as crucial as what you will see and do. So, in addition to the mouth-watering activities such as scenic walks and challenging excursions surrounding Balmoral, diving shipwrecks in Scapa Flow, shopping, clubbing, and dining out, where you settle is crucial.

Where you stay on your first or fiftieth visit to the UK will, to some extent, be an issue of money. However, there are other criteria to consider while selecting a type of lodging in the United Kingdom. How you travel, the number of do-it-yourself you're willing to do, and how you make or don't make friends while on vacation are all variables in deciding where to stay.

4.6.1 Here are a few options for you to consider:

• Hotels

An inexpensive chain hotel could be an adequate and reliable alternative if you're touring and staying one night here and one night there. On the other hand, a country home hotel might be a good alternative if you want a luxury or romantic experience, great food, and much charm for less money than you would pay for equal luxury in a city.

• Vacation Rental Homes

Independent tourists who prefer to prepare their meals and come and go as they please may enjoy vacation house rentals. For families and groups, they're also a good and cost-effective option. And there are many excellent, historic vacation rentals available these days—for example, Agatha Christie's summer home or a 14th-century hall house hidden under brambles fit for Sleeping Beauty.

• Hostels

If you enjoy a welcoming environment and the opportunity to meet new people. A hostel, often known as a "poshtel" these days, might be the answer; they're far more pleasant, clean, and convenient than you might assume, and if you're ready to move on from couch surfing,

• Bed and Breakfast establishments

B&Bs may provide excellent breakfasts, warm and welcoming hosts, convenient locations, and charm without breaking the bank. However, make an informed decision. A dingy B&B with an overbearing or obnoxious landlady might be disastrous. The AA (Automobile Association of the United Kingdom) produces an authoritative directory of the best B&Bs in the UK.

• **House Swap**

To live like a native for free, do a house swap. It's safer and more straightforward than it's ever been. In addition, there are options for house switching in all of the fantastic locales.

• **Camping**

If you enjoy sleeping under the stars, there are plenty of camping options in the UK. All around the UK, there is both wild and caravan camping. The majority of RV parks are open all year.

4.6.2 A cultural and historical perspective on the UK

The United Kingdom has a long and varied history that has seen tribes, kingdoms, empires, and nations rise and fall. As a result, the UK's historic landmarks are as diverse as they are fascinating, ranging from stone-age societies to the Ancient Romans and Norman conquerors to the achievements of the British Empire.

England and the British Isles have a rich tapestry of history that spans thousands of years and is frequently the envy of the globe. From prehistoric persons to the Roman invasion, Saxon Kings, Norman conquests, medieval family feuds, the industrial revolution, and the world's largest global empire.

Its history is apparent from the Scottish border to the north through the English Channel down the south coast. For everyone interested in English history, we've compiled a list of a few must-see historical landmarks.

Historical sites make up some of the most popular tourist destinations in the UK, including the Roman Baths and Edinburgh Castle. Ancient antiquities, medieval castles, and industrial revolution landmarks abound, ensuring that no visit to the UK is complete without historical attractions. There are too many excellent historical sites to list.

The history of the United Kingdom as a developed island nation, a liberal democracy, a major power, and a primarily Christian religious life has influenced its culture. There are customs, cultures, and symbolism unique to each group. Humanism, Catholicism, and the electoral system are all components of wider Western society, and the more magnificent European civilization has influenced British culture. The history of the United Kingdom, its traditionally Christian religious life, its relationship with European cultures, the traditions of England and Ireland, Wales and Scotland, and the impact of the British Empire have impacted British cultural traditions. Even though British culture is distinct, the cultures of England, Scotland, Wales, and Northern Ireland are diverse, with variable degrees of overlap and distinctness among the four countries.

The United Kingdom's literature, songs, filmmaking, art, theatre, comedy, media, and architecture are significant and well worldwide. In addition, food, social etiquette, ceremonies, the arts, holidays, and literature all have traditions and customs that set them apart from other cultures.

Britain is becoming the most culturally fat country in Europe because of its passion for breweries and pub food, consisting mostly of fish and chips on Fridays. The British monarchy still exists, and many of the country's rituals and traditions revolve around the monarchy.

4.7 The United Kingdom's local people
The United Kingdom has many different nationalities, even though everyone is a British citizen. This is since national identity and citizenship are not always synonymous in the United Kingdom.

Despite being British citizens, most white people born in the United Kingdom do not view themselves as British and prefer to identify as English, Scottish, or Welsh. Because diverse groups of people establish their customs and ways of life, there are often noticeable distinctions between people living in each of the United Kingdom's four countries.

Because London is one of the three-nation that makes up the United Kingdom, Scots and Welsh people sometimes become enraged when referred to as "English." They don't live in England and have legislatures, so why should they adopt England's identity? They have their distinct personalities.

English people are from the United Kingdom of Great Britain and Northern Ireland British people, on the other hand, are residents of Great Britain and the United Kingdom.

People born in Scotland are referred to as either Scottish or British, and they can claim to live in Scotland or the United Kingdom. The majority of Scots will identify as Scottish rather than British.

People born in Wales are referred to as either Welsh or British, and they can claim to live in either Wales or the United Kingdom. The majority of Welsh people identify as Welsh rather than British.

4.8 United Kingdom customs and traditions
The United Kingdom has a long history of culture and customs. The customs and traditions of the United Kingdom are well-known worldwide. People often connect Britain with people drinking tea, eating fish and chips, and donning bowler hats, but the country is much more than that. It is a melting pot of cultures and traditions.

The inhabitants of the United Kingdom have a wide range of customs, which include special days and events throughout the year, national holidays, festivals, and celebrations. "Unusual Customs and Traditions Day" is a noteworthy tradition.

4.8.1 Unusual customs and traditions
People would do, eat, or make things they would not normally do on certain days. Festivals such as cheese rolling, nettle consuming, toe combat and bog snorkelling are just some of the oddball, peculiar, quirky, eccentric and even mad celebrations that continue to take place in the United Kingdom to this day.

4.9 The United Kingdom's National Holidays

National Days are not celebrated in Great Britain in the same manner as in other countries.

Only Northern Ireland's (and the Republic of Ireland's) St Patrick's Day and Scotland's St Andrew's Day are official holidays. The rest of the national holidays are regular working days.

Bank Holidays are four public holidays in a year when the government mandates banks and businesses to close. These national Days have no nationalistic or religious significance.

People have called the UK a "superpower of culture," and London has been called the "global cultural capital." The United Kingdom was ranked as the third most positively perceived country in 2017 (after Germany and Canada).

Because the United Kingdom is a multi-national country, there is no singular national costume. Various countries within the United Kingdom, on the other hand, have national costumes or are at least linked to fashion trends. For example, Tam o'shanter and tartan garments are all made in Scotland and feature crisscrossed horizontal and vertical stripes in various colours. In addition, some ladies dress up in traditional Welsh attire, including a Welsh bonnet, for Eisteddfodau.

4.10 The United Kingdom's Art

The United Kingdom inherited the traditions of England, Scotland, and Wales. Arthurian literature and its Welsh roots, William Shakespeare's works, and Scots works such as John Barbour's The Brus.

Since Great Britain was founded in 1707, different visual art linked with the United Kingdom has been referred to as "Art of the United Kingdom." These include English art, Scottish art, Welsh art, and Irish art. During the eighteenth century, Britain began to recapture the dominant position in European art during the Middle Ages, particularly in portraiture and landscape painting.

4.11 The United Kingdom's Cuisine

British cuisine is the specific set of cooking traditions and practices connected with the United Kingdom. Meals created with local condiments of quality, coupled with simple spices to highlight, instead of hiding, the flavour was formerly the definition of British cuisine. International appreciation of British cuisine was limited to the past's full breakfast and Christmas feast. However, Celtic agriculture and animal breeding generated diverse foods for indigenous Celts. Anglo-Saxon England developed beef and delicious herbal stewing techniques before the habit became common in Europe. The Norman conquest brought exotic spices to Britain throughout the Middle Ages. Thanks to the British Empire, people might learn about India's culinary tradition of strong, piercing spices and herbs thanks to the British Empire.

Each country in the United Kingdom has its specialities. However, it is considered the most traditional example of English cuisine. It consists of a roasted piece of meat (typically roast beef, lamb, or chicken) eaten with various vegetables, Yorkshire pudding, and gravy on a Sunday afternoon. The full English breakfast includes bacon, grilled tomatoes, fried bread, baked beans, mushrooms, sausages, and eggs. Black pudding and hash browns are frequently included. A cup of tea or coffee frequently accompanies it. The BBC's Simon Majumdar has named the Ulster fry, which consists of fizzy farl and buckwheat pancakes, the best full breakfast in the UK.

In British food, home baking has always played an important part. A cookbook by food author Eliza Acton titled The Experienced English Housekeeper: Modern Cookery for Private Families started the now-universal practice of stating ingredients and cooking hours for each dish, which is still in use today. The Book of House Maintenance by Isabella Beeton is a well-known British cookbook. Homemade sweets and preserves are part of the traditional English village fête.

4.12 Naming System in British Culture

Everyone in the United Kingdom is given a given name (sometimes known as a "Christian name") and a surname that identifies the child's sex. According to the survey, the British Isles account for almost 90% of names in the dictionaries; the most common in the UK are Jones, William, Smith, Taylor, Johnson, Brown, and Park.

Middle names have become increasingly popular during the nineteenth century and sometimes derive from a family member's name.

The majority of surnames with a UK origin fall into one of seven groups:

Occupation, e.g., Sawyer, Brewer, Cooper, Cook, Carpenter, Bailey, Parker, Forrester, Palmer, Archer, Taylor, Turner, Knight, Slater, Weaver, Wright.

Personal features, e.g., Brown, Young, Black, Whitehead, Stout, Long, Short, White.

Geographical features, e.g., Forest, Sound, Bridge, Camp, Fields, Moore, Wood, Holmes, Underwood, Hall, Brooks, Stone, Morley, and Perry.

Places, e.g., Murray, Everingham, Hamilton, Sutton, Flint, and Laughton.

The name of **their lands or estate**, for those derived from landowners.

Ancestral surnames are derived from a person's given name, for example, a male character: Richardson, Jones, Williams, Thomas, Jackson, Wilson, Thompson, Murphy, Nicholson, Robinson, Powell, Ferguson, Davis, Edwards, Harrison, Watson, or female names Molson, Gilson, Emmott (from Emma), Marriott (from Mary).

CHAPTER 5 GOLFING IN A THE UK CITY

Golf is one of the sports that people in the United Kingdom play the most. England has the most golf courses in Europe, with 1,872, followed by Germany with 731, less than half of that number. Scotland has 560 golf courses, 405 in Ireland, and 145 in Wales. However, the proportion of golf resorts in the United Kingdom has continuously dropped compared to other countries.

Scotland and Ireland are often cited as some of the best golf destinations globally, but the United States is sometimes overlooked as the best golf destination globally. The championship courses available in England are astounding, ranging from gorgeous yet challenging link courses along the coast to serene parkland or heathland courses.

England also boasts the most registered golfers in Europe, with over 656 thousand players, barely ahead of Germany, with over 645 thousand players. In addition, there are 188 thousand golfers registered in Scotland, 183 thousand in Ireland, and 45 thousand in Wales.

England's 946 thousand regular golfers have remained largely constant, regardless of intensity or duration or how often they play.

You'll find historical sites and breath-taking scenery in the British Isles, with each country and destination offering something unique. A golf trip to the UK and Ireland offers lots of diversity, with thousands of courses to pick from, ranging from links and clifftop to heathland and parkland.

The 'Home of Golf,' Scotland, is unquestionably the flagship country and a must-see for any golfer, closely followed by Ireland, which offers a superb mix of links between golf and renowned hospitality. There are other Open Championship venues in England, and Wales, despite its lesser-known status, is a terrific alternative for golfers looking for hidden jewels.

However, there are several peculiarities to playing golf in the United Kingdom or Ireland that you should know before boarding a plane or stepping onto the first tee of a typical golf course in the British Isles. Here are our top five suggestions for organizing your golf trip to the United Kingdom or Ireland.

1. Walking the course; many courses in the United Kingdom and Ireland prohibit buggy use - unless you have a medical condition, you will have trouble walking. Thankfully, the more commercial golf courses provide buggies; if a buggy ride is something that appeals to you, make sure to inquire and reserve one ahead of time. The good news is that most courses have pull trollies accessible, which will undoubtedly assist.

2. Request caddies ahead of time; some courses do provide caddies, but you must request them ahead of time. They are worth the money if you are willing to pay because they will improve your scorecard and playing experience while also filling your day with humorous and engaging stories. The cost of a caddy usually is around £50 - £75 per round.

3. Both possibilities are self-serve driving ranges and clubs that don't even have driving ranges, simply a practice mat and net. In the old days, the golfing nobility of the period did not consider it necessary to warm up - instead, they hit a few balls over the fen before their game and then asked their servants to pick them up. Instead of driving directly from the car to the first tee, I recommend that you check ahead of time whether a course has a driving range, and if it doesn't, arrive slightly earlier and make sure you loosen up with some good old stretches, rather than driving straight from the car to the first tee.

4. In-Out course layouts are standard in the UK, with many courses having nine holes in and nine holes out (with the 9th being the furthest point from the Clubhouse). While some more commercial courses feature halfway homes, others do not, and those that do are rarely open to the public. Be prepared to play the entire 18 holes without stopping, which can be exhausting if you are not adequately prepared.

5. *Bring your refreshments,* whether it's a hip flask, an energy drink, or a sandwich, as there's unlikely a cart lady or boy racing around the fairways at your beck and call offering you delights.

6. *There are no restrooms on the course,* either before or after. Alternatively, it'll be a trip to the bushes for you! To avoid any embarrassing or unpleasant circumstances, make sure this is crucial for your pre-round preparations.

7. *Some clubs may require a jacket and tie in the Clubhouse;* if this is the case, embrace it and enjoy the traditional atmosphere while socializing with the locals. You'll undoubtedly receive a warm welcome and hear some incredible stories.

8. *The climate:* Even at the height of summer, you can experience four seasons in a single day in the United Kingdom; this means bringing some decent rain gear and possibly a spare pair of shoes. However, don't bother with a brolly because modern science has yet to invent a links golf umbrella that can withstand a 25-knot side wind. You will also save weight in your suitcase by not bringing it.

5.1 Best Golf Courses or Golf Vacation Destinations in England

Some of the best golf vacation destinations globally are located in the United Kingdom and Ireland. Ireland is home to over a quarter of the world's natural links courses, each with its distinct personality. Then there's Wales, which boasts miles of lovely shoreline and acres of unspoiled countryside brimming with hidden beauties.

5.1.1 Coast of Kent

There are several Championship links on the Kent coast, and the sweeping dunes of Southport are home to some of the best courses in the country. Scotland's stunning, natural landscape appears to have been created specifically to generate golf courses of exceptional beauty and challenge.

5.1.2 Royal County Down

It was named top on Golfers Digest's biennial list in 2016 and 2018. Many people believe the golf course in the Murlough National Nature Reserve, which runs along Dundrum Bay and is surrounded by the gorgeous Mourne Mountains, to be the most spectacularly beautiful in the world.

Don't be misled by Royal County Down's beauty; the course is a true golf test, with narrow fairways and 'bearded bunkers' requiring superb ball control.

5.1.3 The golf club of Royal Birkdale

It's in the Lancashire town of Royal Birkdale. Royal Birkdale Golf Club has a long and distinguished history with nine Open Championships, two Ryder Cups, and many other tournaments, including the Walker Cup and the Women's British Open.

The course is placed 15th on Golf Digest's list for 2018. If you're a golfer, you must play Royal Birkdale, possibly England's most prestigious golf course.

5.1.4 West Midlands

The Ryder Cup, British Masters, English Open, and a slew of other European Tour tournaments have all been held in the West Midlands, demonstrating its status as a top golfing destination.

Birmingham is one of the liveliest cities in the area, with lots of bars, restaurants, and off-course activities to keep you occupied while you're not on the fairways.

5.1.5 London and the South East

Kent is a popular destination for golfers due to the abundance of superb golf courses crammed into a small area.

South East London spans a vast area, and although links golf abounds in Kent, Sussex, Surrey, and Hertfordshire offer a diverse range of exquisite inland courses to suit any golf group and budget.

East Sussex National, Hanbury Manor, Foxhills Golf Resort, and Kent are the best golf courses and golf resorts for a golf trip in South East England.

5.1.6 East Midlands

Many golf courses are located in the East Midlands, many of which are in England's Top 100. From Nottingham's Notts Golf Club and its mature woodland appeal to Lincolnshire's Woodhall Spa, which was created by Harry Vardon and updated by Harry Colt.

Breadsall Priory, Hellidon Lakes, Belton Woods, Nottingham, and others are among the best golf courses and golf resorts in the East Midlands.

Wentworth in England, Celtic Manor in Wales, Carnoustie in Scotland, and Ancient Golf Club of Saint Andrews are well-known golf courses in the United Kingdom.

5.2 The Best Hotels in the UK with Golf Courses

5.2.1 Bovey Castle

The spectacular setting of Bovey Castle, which overlooks lushly covered hills on the western edge of Dartmoor National Park, is breathtaking. It's the perfect base for various "country sports," including hunting, shooting, fishing, and golfing on the 18-hole championship course. There's a heated pool and whirlpool on the premises and a small spa and gym. The rooms are warm and inviting, with decanters of estate-made sloe gin.

5.2.2 The Fairmont St Andrews

Fairmont St Andrews is a luxury 5* hotel perched majestically on the cliffs above St Andrews Bay, overlooking two superb championship golf courses and the famed St Andrews skyline.

The resort is just 10 minutes from St Andrews Links and the world-famous Kingsbarns and is located on Scotland's stunning east coast, just 90 minutes from Edinburgh.

5.2.3 Druids Glen Golf Resort

The resort, located in the gorgeous Wicklow Hills to the south of Dublin, features two championship golf courses, a five-star hotel, and an award-winning spa. Many great golfers have compared the four-time Irish Open Druids Glen Course to Augusta National, and the relatively new Druids Heath course has hosted the Irish PGA Championship.

5.2.4 Turnberry Resort by Trump

The Trump Turnberry Resort, situated on some of Scotland's most stunning coastline, will give a unique golfing experience. The 5-star hotel or the self-catering cottages and villas are available to guests. Turnberry's courses are spectacular, with the Ailsa course serving as the main attraction, having held four Open Championships. Trump Turnberry is also the Open, Senior Open, and Women's Open site and was named Europe's Best Golf Resort for 2019.

5.2.5 Carton House Hotel & Golf Club

Carton House and its two golf championship courses, just 30 minutes from Dublin, have quickly become one of Ireland's most opulent golfing destinations.

The majestic Palladian house is set in 1000 acres of the Irish countryside. It is surrounded by two fantastic courses: the Montgomerie course, which has hosted many Irish Opens, and the lovely O'Meara Course.

5.2.6 Hotel, Golf, and Spa at Rockcliffe Hall

The 5-star Rockcliffe Hall hotel, located in County Durham in the heart of the North West of England, offers world-class elegance, outstanding spa and leisure facilities, and superb food. The Martin Hawtree golf course is one of Europe's longest at 7,879 yards, but golfers of all abilities can play thanks to five different sets of tees.

5.3 Important guidelines for every golfer

Golfers concentrate on the game for 4-5 hours at a time. Compared to an hour of intense competition focusing on other sports, that's a lot of energy and calories to burn. Aside from physical and mental preparation, many serious athletes consider their food and its impact on total performance essential.

5.3.1 Take some time to relax. On the eve of a tournament

Sleep is essential for golfers' mental and physical health, so set aside your studies and activities to relax the night before a competition. To help you relax, go to bed early and do some breathing exercises and mental preparation.

5.3.2 Drink plenty of water

Forget about sugary sports drinks and energy drinks. When it comes to staying hydrated, water reigns supreme! On the golf course, it can get quite hot. Dehydration can impair muscular performance and make it difficult to concentrate. It might also damage your energy levels, making you feel sluggish and lethargic. Ensure you have a water bottle with you during the competition. Drink 16 fl oz of water before your round and another 8 Fl oz 20 minutes before your game.

5.3.3 Foods to eat before and during a golf game

Protein shakes: Protein shakes are a practical and quick-acting approach to keep you fueled on the golf course. Open it and go. According to nutritionist Marc Halpern, plant-based protein smoothies with vegetable and fruit extracts are the best for golfers.

The organ is one brand he recommends because of its fruits and vegetables, which he finds healthier than others.

Bananas and apples: "An apple a day keeps the doctor away," as the adage goes. Similarly, a round of apples or bananas keeps the bogeys at bay. According to Halpern, they are two of the easiest fruits to eat and tolerate. Both can be readily sliced into bite-sized portions and eaten. Berries are also a good fruit alternative. Apples and bananas, on the other hand, are Halpern's favourites.

Almonds: Bring almonds if you want to nibble like Phil Mickelson. For around, they're a good, healthy alternative. On the other hand, almonds are excellent when combined with other nuts and fruits. Because trail mix is a high-calorie snack, Halpern advises golfers to make their own.

Sandwiches with peanut butter: Peanut butter sandwiches are abundant in protein and carbohydrates. Put on a little jelly, and you're good to go. According to Halpern, the only issue with peanut butter sandwiches is that they lack fibre. As a result, it may burn quickly, increasing hunger on the course. However, the old PB&J is a safe bet in general.

Snickers: Snickers are a simple, easy, and quick snack on the course that will keep you full for around. Snickers can also deliver energy to golfers when they need it the most.

5.3.4 Avoid these foods before and during your golf game

The right foods and beverages will provide your body and mind with the nutrition they require to compete effectively. Here are some suggestions for reshaping your diet in preparation for your next golf event.

What you put into your body is crucial, and the appropriate nutrients will provide you with the energy you need to win the tournament. Say no to starchy carbs like doughnuts and pancakes, which will merely give a sugar high followed by a collapse in energy. Oatmeal, pasta, and bread are all excellent examples of whole-wheat foods. Combine with lean meats like chicken and eggs and fruits and green vegetables. Eat a snack before heading to the first tee, and eat at least 2-3 hours before the round.

One common thing among all players is that we all enjoy eating. Before, during, and following around. While some snacks can help you stay energized and focused, others can deplete your vitality.

Cheetos/Doritos: Cheetos and Doritos are bad if you don't eat them properly. Your ball, clubs, and glove may turn orange if you don't wash your hands after eating. The greatest nightmare of a golfer. Doritos and Cheetos are essentially salty junk food from a health standpoint.

Golfers should avoid citrus fruits on the course since they are more acidic and generally irritating than apples and bananas. Of course, many golfers may be completely comfortable with them. Food "backfiring" on you when standing over a birdie putt is the last thing you need. If at all possible, stay away from citrus fruits.

Hot dogs: Hot dogs are a terrific alternative for convenience. It's a quick and easy meal that will keep you going till the 19th hole. At the halfway house, they're very seductive.

Heavy foods: This is a big category, but the answer is simple: don't eat anything serious before or during a round of golf. Leave the 19th hole to them. Pancake breakfasts, burgers, steaks, nachos, and French fries are among them. Processed foods sap your energy and make it difficult to focus on your game. Consequently, you're less likely to perform well when your energy level drops.

CHAPTER 6: CITIES IN THE UNITED KINGDOM

Currently, the United Kingdom has 70 cities: 52 in England, seven in Scotland, Wales has six, and five in Ireland. Lord Mayors is found in 23 cities across England, two in Wales, and two in Northern Ireland; Lord Provosts is located in four cities across Scotland. In some circumstances, the city-status area does not correspond to the built-up area or conurbation it belongs. The City of London has city status in Greater London. Still, no other local authority, nor Greater London, has been awarded city status. In certain circumstances, such as the Cities of Canterbury and Lancaster, the designation refers to a local government district that encompasses several towns and rural areas outside of the major settlement.

The majority of people in the United Kingdom live in cities. Only 22% of the population resided in rural areas in 1960. This percentage dropped to just 17% in 2015, on the lower end of the rural population scale. Many factors contribute to the United Kingdom's population increase in major cities, including the country's rich culture and history, growing economies, and educational and career possibilities across the country's numerous industries.

The United Kingdom has one city with more than one million people, 95 cities with a population of 100,000 to one million people, and 951 cities with a population of 10,000 to 100,000 people. London has been recorded to be the largest city in the UK.

England's cities;

- Bath
- Carlisle
- Chelmsford
- Coventry
- Derby
- Durham
- Ely
- Exeter
- Hull
- Leeds
- Leicester
- Lincoln
- Liverpool
- London, England
- Manchester
- Newcastle-upon-Tyne
- Norwich
- Nottingham
- Oxford
- Peterborough
- Plymouth
- Portsmouth
- Preston
- Ripon
- Salford
- Salisbury
- Sheffield
- Southend-On-Sea
- Southampton
- St Albans
- Stoke-on-Trent
- Sunderland
- Truro
- Wakefield

- Wells
- Westminster City Council
- Winchester
- York

Cities in Scotland;
- Inverness
- Perth
- Dundee
- Stirling
- Aberdeen
- Edinburgh
- Glasgow

Cities in Wales

- Bangor
- Cardiff
- Newport
- St. Asaph's
- The Cathedral Close and St Davids
- Swansea

Cities in Northern Ireland
- Lisburn
- Belfast
- Derry
- Armagh
- Newry.

6.1 Top cities in the United Kingdom and their attractions

The United Kingdom house a lot of the world's beautiful cities. Whether it's London's theatrical and shopping areas of Edinburgh's medieval streets, our cities are fascinating attractions in their own right. Beyond that, many exciting and unusual places don't skimp on delicious food or fascinating attractions.

6.1.1 London
London is a world centre of art, performing art, songs, culture, and literature. It houses the Houses of Parliament, The British Museum, The Tower of London, Westminster Abbey, and other top English monuments; the city is a cosmopolitan city with vibrant markets, excellent shopping, and diverse culture.

London house up to 7.5 million people, approximately 12.5% of the population of the United Kingdom, Moreover, 1.5 million Londoners are foreign-born, not including visitors. They can communicate in 300 different languages.

6.1.2 Manchester
Manchester is widely referred to as the world's first modern metropolis; it was once the world's cotton capital and one of the industrial revolution's breeding grounds in the 18th century. Manchester's industrial tycoons funded museums, galleries, theatres, libraries, and exceptional structures. After a deadly IRA explosion in 1996, city centre renovation became necessary, culminating in a new, spectacular 21st-century cityscape.

Manchester and the surrounding Salford Quays neighbourhood now have some fascinating architecture in the United Kingdom. Bridgewater Hall, Urbis, and the Imperial War Museum, created by Daniel Libeskind, are just a few attractions.

The independent and mainstream music sectors have long thrived in Manchester. Elkie Brooks, Freddie, the Dreamers, Herman's Hermits, Morrissey, and hundreds more are among the bands and musicians who started in Manchester city.

Manchester's club culture is thriving, mainly to the city's large student population. In addition, because it is one of the gateways to England's Lake District, Manchester makes for an excellent starting point for a two-base trip that combines natural activities with urban nightlife.

6.1.3 Edinburgh

Located in the heart of Scotland's capital city and Parliament, Edinburgh combines the youthful and contemporary tastes of a large university city and seat of government with a historically significant and gorgeous setting to create a unique and memorable experience for visitors. Arthur's Seat, a mountain in the centre of town, is home to the world's largest performing arts festival, a 1,000year-old castle, and the world's largest performing arts festival. And Hogmanay, Edinburgh's traditional New Year's celebration, is unlike any four-day street carnival.

Edinburgh has a population of over 500,000 people, including 62,000 university students. At least 13 million individuals visit each year. During the previous festival month of August, Edinburgh's population grows by almost a million people.

From late June to early September, Scotland is a frenzy of festivities. Film, books, art, music, television, jazz, the Royal Edinburgh Military Tattoo, and the Edinburgh International Festival are among the summer festivals. However, the main event is the Edinburgh Fringe, a free-for-all of drama, music, comedy, and street theatre that varies greatly in quality and takes over the entire city for most of August.

Hogmanay, the world's largest New Year's celebration, returns to Edinburgh in the winter months. Four days of festivities include a torchlight procession, fire festival, music, funfair, and winter swimming.

6.1.4 Birmingham

Birmingham was Britain's manufacturing hub for most of the nineteenth and twentieth centuries, thanks to entrepreneurship and engineering prowess.

Birmingham has several delectable claims to fame. George Cadbury created his chocolates, and his Bourneville Estate was a pioneering planned town. Moreover, Birmingham has recently emerged as the epicentre of the Anglo-Punjabi speciality known as Balti food.

Birmingham is the UK's second-largest city, with over a million people. It's a bustling, multi-ethnic city with thriving art and music scene and some of the best shopping in England. Its Selfridges, the company's first store outside of London, is a futuristic structure that appears to have landed from space.

Birmingham is known for its heavy metal sound; Black Sabbath and Judas Priest are local bands. Ozzie Osborne, on the other hand, is a native son. Birmingham is also a hotbed for different types of music. Duran, ELO, and UB40 all had their start in the city.

Birmingham attracts many visitors due to its excellent shopping and the massive NEC convention facility. But, unfortunately, there aren't nearly enough hotels to fulfil the demand. So, if you're going there for a particular occasion, make a reservation as soon as possible.

6.1.4 Oxford

Oxford Institution, founded in the 11th century, is England's oldest university. It's why so many people go to this small town on the border of the Cotswold's, 60 miles northwest of London.

The Ashmolean, England's oldest public museum, was recently renovated. Visitors can also go shopping in a bustling covered market, see a haunted castle, and find an almost hidden bar popular when Elizabeth Taylor and Richard Burton were still hiding their affair from their respective husbands.

Then there are the colleges, of course. Most colleges' magnificent, ancient grounds and chapels are open to visitors. Some are only open at specific periods of the day or as part of organized trips. The Oxford Tourist Information Centre offers official guided walking tours that allow you to see the attractions at college, including some well-known landmarks and movie locations. Some of the places from the Harry Potter films may even be seen.

Oxford is a fantastic day trip from London, whether you have a car. It's also an excellent point to start exploring the Cotswold's, seeing Blenheim Palace in Woodstock (a ten-minute bus ride away), and shopping until you drop at Bicester Village, one of the top designer's bargain shops in the UK.

6.1.4 Glasgow

In terms of tourists and visitors, Glasgow, Scotland's largest metropolis and the UK's third-largest city, had long been overshadowed by Edinburgh. People were put off by its reputation as a rough, crime-ridden, filthy, and hard-drinking city. On the other hand, Glaswegians have worked hard to change that image since the mid-1980s.

The UK government changed Glasgow's name to the European Capital of Culture in 1995. The award was given for a completely different vibe than the heritage culture that animates Edinburgh. It's only getting better. Glasgow was designated one of the top ten tourist destinations by Lonely Planet in 2008. The Mercer study, quality of life survey, ranked Glasgow among the world's top 50 safest cities in the same year. Tourists on the edge of their seats should be aware that this was more than 30 places higher than London.

Billy Connolly's hometown is now a trendy hangout for modern art, jazz, nightclubs, comedy, design, and fashion.

6.1.5 Bristol

Bristol is a tiny, picturesque city on the boundary of Somerset and Gloucestershire with a history of creativity and invention. It provides an excellent tourist base with Warwick Castle, Bath, Stonehenge, Stratford-upon-Avon, Cheddar Gorge, and Longleat within reasonable driving distance.

In the 17th and 18th centuries, it was a hub for the triangle trade, which involved selling produced goods to Africa in exchange for enslaved people who were subsequently forcibly relocated to the Americas. Thomas Clarkson, an abolitionist, lived in secret at The Seven Stars Pub in Thomas Lane in the 18th century. He obtained slave trade intelligence for his friend William Wilberforce, who used it to support the Anti-Slavery Act. The tavern, which has been serving authentic ale since 1760 and dates back to the 1600s, is still open every day.

For ages, Bristol has been a hive of inventive minds. Brunel designed the Great Western Railway, which connected London and Bristol and the SS Great Britain, the world's first ocean-going, propeller-driven transatlantic steamship. The Clifton Railway Bridge was completed after his death. The bridge that spans the Avon Gorge is the city's icon.

The Bristol Old Vic, a branch of London's Old Vic Theatre, and its accompanying drama school have produced graduates who have graced international stages and screens. Patrick Stewart, Greta Scacchi, Jeremy Irons, Miranda Richardson, Helen Baxendale, Daniel Day-Lewis, and Gene Wilder were born and raised in Bristol.

Aardman Animation's Wallace & Gromit and Shaun the Sheep are also Bristol locals, having been conceived there. In addition, Banksy, a secretive graffiti artist from Bristol, has left his imprint there.

6.1.6 Newcastle-upon-Tyne

Tyne began its existence as an important Roman fort guarding Hadrian's Wall's eastern end. The evidence is still on display at the Arbeia Roman Fort & Museum, including a replica of the defence that guarded Tyne's mouth and exhibitions featuring archaeological findings from the site.

Following the Romans' departure, the Venerable Bede, an Anglo-Saxon monk, lived and wrote his history of early Britain at Jarrow, on the south bank of the Tyne, just downriver from Newcastle. Jarrow Hall (previously Bede's World), amid the remnants of Bede's Anglo-Saxon abbey, is a new museum and World Heritage Site candidate in Jarrow.

Newcastle is a fantastic starting point for touring the northeast of England, but don't be shocked if the locals are unconcerned about the city's rich past. Instead, they are entirely focused on now and tomorrow.

Newcastle's nightlife is famed, producing many bands, performers, and good times. Sting is a Geordie, and Dire Straits is a Newcastle band. Newcastle is home to the "Geordies." Newcastle is one of England's major university cities, and students keep the music industry alive and well.

The Newcastle Quays have been turned into a modern and artistic landscape since the Millennium. For example, the Millennium Bridge in Newcastle/Gateshead is a one-of-a-kind pedestrian "drawbridge." Rather than splitting and opening to enable tall boat traffic, the bridge's lowest pedestrian deck tips up to meet the support arch and doorway and shuts like an eyelid.

On the quayside, the Baltic Centre for Contemporary Art is a massive contemporary art facility and the world's most significant exhibition space of its sort. Before transforming into a cutting-edge visual arts exhibition facility, it was an immense and abandoned flour and animal feed mill. The Sage Gateshead is an advanced music performance and study centre not far away. Inside Sage's dazzling stainless steel and glass bubbles, rock, pop, indie, country, folk, electronic, dance, and world music are all performed. In addition, the Sage is home to Northern Sinfonia.

Geordies; Newcastle's native dialect, Geordie, is distinct and one of England's oldest. You've probably heard this unique accent from actors Jimmy Nail and Cheryl Cole of Girls Aloud.

6.1.7 Liverpool
The Beatles may spring to mind when visitors think of Liverpool. And, of course, there are plenty of Beatles-related activities to partake in, not least a visit to the legendary Cavern Club.

The European Capital of Culture title was bestowed on Liverpool in 2008, rejuvenating the city in England's northwest, as such awards frequently do. In addition, the Albert Docks district of Liverpool was designated as a UNESCO World Heritage Site for its significance in British maritime history. Visitors to the region can learn about Liverpool's role in the slave trade and the spread of culture and business and culture across the British Empire. In addition to trendy clubs, hotels, shopping, dining, and a Liverpool branch of the famous Tate Gallery, the attention to the dock's history has drawn stylish clubs, shopping, dining, and hotels.

6.1.8 Cambridge
Like its traditional rival Oxford, Cambridge evolved from a gathering of academics who organized institutions from one spot. According to mythology, Cambridgeshire was created in 1209 after a party of scholars left Oxford due to a disagreement with the locals.

Despite being smaller and less urban than Oxford, Cambridge is a vibrant city with excellent museums and galleries, theatres, restaurants, and bars. The colleges themselves are architectural marvels from the Middle Ages, Tudors, and Jacobeans. With its high arching vaulted ceiling, Kings College Chapel is a must-see among the attractions available to visitors.

Between April and September, Cambridge can be overwhelmed by tourists who arrive by bus, stay for a few hours, and then go. However, because rail services from London are frequent and journey times are short, a trip to the Back would be incomplete without visiting some exquisite gardens. Because of the crowds, numerous universities have started charging an admission fee and limiting their operating hours.

6.2 Putting a Bet on a Punt

Punts are classic flatboats that float down the Cam and Grantchester rivers, pushed by poles. The punter takes a step forward and drives the bar into the muck. It's not as simple as it appears! As the punt floats on, more than one newbie has either lost a pole or been left clutching to one. Visitors can now book a chauffeured punt for a guided trip along the Backs (the chauffeur will most likely be a student). It's low-key, but it's much fun.

One of Cambridge's flaws is the scarcity of genuinely great hotels in the city centre. The Moller Centre, part of Churchill College, is one of the most intriguing. It's primarily a conference facility, although anyone can stay in business class luxury for a reasonable fee in this architecturally unique location.

CHAPTER 7: DISCOVERING ENTICING GETAWAYS IN THE UK

Exchanging far-flung destinations for excursions to lesser-known parts of Britain appears to be increasingly a win-win situation, from the Isle of Skye to the Isles of Scilly. Fortunately, luxurious destination hotels have sprung up all over the country in recent years, from Kent to Aberdeen, and each one is a delight to visit in any season.

If you know where to look, Britain can compete with the sophisticated European towns we like. There are rolling hills, seashore fish and chips, and a plethora of pasties to be found here. Some hotels have reopened, and vacation cottages and campgrounds are now taking bookings. So if you have any unused annual leave or want to take a weekend getaway, the crucial British holiday is worth considering.

Art lovers should head north to Braemar, where Hauser & Wirth's founders opened the Fife Arms, just nine miles from Balmoral. At the same time, dedicated foodies should visit The Newt in Somerset, the sister hotel of South Africa's Eden-like Babylonstoren. What are the best couples' trips in the United Kingdom? The Pig in Harlyn Bay offers romantic seclusion, while Heckfield Place in Hampshire offers unparalleled indulgence.

You must first pick where you want to go. Within a few hours of London, you can enjoy miles and miles of unspoiled coastline and beautiful and picturesque villages. Cornwall, Devon, and the Gower Peninsula's gorgeous shoreline are worth visiting, especially in the cooler months. The UK's lovely cities are usually more attractive in the autumn.

7.1 UK Getaway Cities

7.1.1 The Peak District

In the past, comfortable pubs with blazing log fireplaces have been the most incredible places to stay in the Peak District. However, the converted Victorian pile Callow Hall is the most beautiful spot to put your head after a day of strolling as of 2021. Guests can select from discreet rooms in the main house with solitary copper baths or genuinely immerse themselves in the countryside in one of the "treehouse" or "hive" suites designed by the Chewton Glen team. The grounds, though, are so wonderful that you'd be tempted to stay in your room for more than a few hours, lovely as they are: Callow Hall's 35 acres feature ancient wild streams, woodlands, and fruit orchards, not to mention rolling lawns where visitors may play croquet.

While the appealing cuisine at Callow Hall's on-site restaurant is based on seasonal British produce (including grouse from August 12th), a picnic atop a limestone cliff is a must-do while visiting the Peak District. Combine a visit to Chatsworth with a stop at the Estate Farm Shop, which sells local meats, cheeses, and pieces of bread.

Follow the Lathkill Dale, a narrow, rocky ravine, to Haddon Hall, a 900-year-old medieval home with a rose-filled Elizabethan Garden, one of Britain's best surviving medieval homes.

7.1.2 Northumberland

The Lord Crewe Arms, located in the honey-stoned village of Blanchland, began life as a 12th-century monastery before becoming one of Northumberland's most beautiful hotels. Stained-glass windows and massive fireplaces are among the many relics of the past that tourists can still find. The rooms are charming, packed with tattered paperbacks, hot-water bottles, and unusual fudge. They are spread across the main building, a former tavern across the road, and many miners' cottages. Guests can borrow all they need to enjoy the nearby countryside, including Wellington boots and fishing equipment on the hotel's stretch of the River Derwent.

Make a Sunday lunch reservation at the on-site restaurant, including a glass of Crewe Brew Ale.

There were always enchanted food lovers at Riley's Fish Shack when it initially opened as a mobile stall in 2012; its speciality is (of course) the catch of the day, which can range from lobster to monkfish served with crispy potatoes that make you want to sing. Oh, and hot buttered rum brewed right there on the premises.

7.1.3 Pembrokeshire

The Grove in Narberth is undoubtedly one of Wales's most attractive hotels, set in 26 acres of trees and meadows, with the Preseli Hills just visible in the distance on clear days. The hotel's Arts & Crafts-inspired rooms are warm and inviting, featuring deep roll-top bathrooms in several suites. The upstairs sitting room with a blazing log fire (and plenty of novels to read if it rains) and the scented walled gardens on the property are also really charming.

The Fernery, the Grove's much-lauded restaurant, uses hyper-local food to highlight the finest of Welsh cuisine: Fermented leeks in onion soup; Eccles cake, according to Las. Next, head to the charmingly unusual Café Môr for a considerably less formal but uniquely special lunch of lobster rolls with Welsh Sea butter and Welshman's caviar.

From Prescipe Bay Church to Doors Cove, with its fossil-studded sandstone cliffs, once the domain of smugglers, Pembrokeshire has a solid claim for some of the most beautiful beaches in the UK. Take a boat to the Ramsey Islands, home to peregrines, seals, and other wildlife.

7.1.4 Somerset

The Newt, naturally named after its resident colony of great crested newts, is the only Somerset hotel worth visiting right now. The spacious 17th-century estate has exquisite Georgian-inspired suites in the main house, Hadspen House, and intimate, more rustic lodging in the former stable yard, designed by the couple behind the famed Babylonstoren in Stellenbosch. However, the beautiful gardens, which feature a Baroque-style maze, ancient trees, and wild swimming ponds, are the main reason to visit.

Visit Hauser & Wirth Somerset, which showcases world-class exhibitions throughout the year, then dine at the on-site Roth Bar & Grill, whose menu is inspired by the vegetables from the surrounding Durslade Farm and its kitchen garden. Their free-range pork chops are exceptional, having been dry-cured in their own Salt Room.

Wells Cathedral is home to over 300 Gothic sculptures, spectacular scissor arches, and one of the world's oldest clock movements.

7.1.5 Norfolk

It's more challenging to get a more beautiful place to stay in Norfolk than Hales Hall. The medieval estate's rooms are spread among five separate buildings, the oldest of which was erected in 1478. Each room has its unique character, but expect four-poster beds and open fires. So what is Vogue's favourite hangout spot? With a secluded walled garden, the rose-covered Cottage. Take a walk in the Norfolk Broads National Park, which features hundreds of miles of rivers, uncommon bird species, and wildflowers, to escape the magnificent interiors.

A pub in Norfolk, The Gunton Arms' walls are adorned with works by Damien Hirst, Lucian Freud, and Tracey Emin, yet the restaurant's delectable food will still dominate the conversation. Order the venison from Gunton Hall's 18th-century deer park and a selection of traditional British puddings such as blackberry jelly with ice cream and buttermilk pudding with honeyed figs.

Explore Norwich's Cathedral Quarter, a maze of cobblestoned alleyways lined with medieval buildings, before visiting the city's traditional open-air market, one of the country's oldest.

7.1.6 Cornwall

The Pig's Cornwall property in Harlyn Bay, set within a 15th-century mansion west of Padstow, boasts everything its hotels are known for, including a "25-mile" meal with Newlyn turbot and Porthilly mussels, matched with organic vegetables and fresh herbs from the kitchen garden. For a true sense of being completely immersed in nature, choose one of the Garden Wagons on the grounds instead of a room in the Main House. In the summer, a walk through a poppy field leads to the thundering surf of Constantine Bay, yet it's just as tempting to spend a whole day at the Potting Shed spa.

Fitzroy is run by the same team behind London favourites Primeur and Westerns Laundry and is located in Fowey, a regular source of inspiration for Daphne du Maurier. During summer, the menu changes daily but is focused on sharing dishes; in the winter, head chef Ethan Friskney-Bryer hosts supper clubs and pop-ups at Fitzroy's more informal sister location, North Street Kitchen.

Nothing beats witnessing Barbara Hepworth's modernist sculptures in her St Ives home garden, where she lived and worked for over 25 years, drawing inspiration from the beautiful Cornish light.

7.1.7 The Brecon Beacons are a group of mountains in Wales

Wales, like Scotland, is a fantastic destination for couples, especially adventurous couples. The Brecon Beacons in south Wales are popular destinations for couples and easily accessible from major cities such as London and Cardiff. You'll never run out of things to do in this hiker's paradise, from hiking and biking to camping and even stargazing.

It's simple to get out into the hills and walk along with one of the many well-marked routes. The stunning Four Falls climb takes in the park's most scenic waterfalls: Cwm Porth and the Eira falls, one of the most popular. An enjoyable hike can take upwards of four hours.

The 90-foot Henry Falls is another attractive waterfall to visit. It's the country's tallest fall, and it's a reasonably straightforward climb that even people with modest stamina may enjoy.

7.1.8 London, United Kingdom

England's capital has world-class museums, West End plays, and premier art galleries for short getaways in the UK. London attracts the biggest names in music, sport, and the arts with a crowded roster of exhibitions and events throughout the year. It also doesn't have to be expensive; many of the capital's institutions are free, and low-cost events are offered all year. It was just voted the world's most incredible city by Rough Guides readers. There will never be a time when you don't have something to do here.

7.1.9 Llandudno is a Welsh town

The sweeping curve of Llandudno's bay lures visitors year after year, and it's easy to see why: the seaside town boasts breath-taking coastline beauty. Board the tramway to the top of Great Orme for a spectacular view of the bay. Alternatively, ride one of the town's cable cars to get a bird's eye view of the action. Finally, climb the battlements of nearby Conwy Castle to enjoy the snow-capped mountains of Snowdonia and the tranquil Conwy estuary.

7.2 United Kingdom's Seasons

The season of the United Kingdom is among the most significant pieces of knowledge that anyone travelling to the United Kingdom to explore, cruise, or have the most enjoyable adventure. Knowing the seasons ahead of time will assist travellers in determining the ideal time of year to travel and possible activities throughout specific seasons.

Although not as severe as in other countries, the UK has a significant difference in summers and winters. The year is divided into four seasons, each lasting around three months. The seasons frequently overlap or do not follow a predictable pattern due to the notoriously changeable British weather.

Winter is the coldest season in the UK, lasting roughly from December to February. Morning frost, ice on car windscreens and streets, and snowfall are common when temperatures fall below freezing (0 degrees Celcius). Winters in the UK are generally wet and windy, so bring a warm, waterproof coat. During the winter, daylight hours are severely reduced, and weekdays in London are dipping as low as 8 hours towards the end of the month.

The winter seasons consist of the coldest months with the shortest days. Winter weather in the UK may be highly different; most winters see the storminess of fall continue with lots of rain and wind; in fact, the UK often experiences some of the most significant winds throughout the winter. Winters in other parts of the world are much colder and calmer, with plenty of fog, frost, and even snow. Some winters are a combination of the two, depending on where you reside. People who live in the south of the United Kingdom or near the coasts will likely have milder winters than those in the north of the country or far from the beaches.

The winter solstice occurs when the northern hemisphere gets tilted away from the Sun. Every year on the 21st or 22nd of December, we have our shortest day and longest night.

The weather in July and May will be pleasant and sunny, with stunning sunsets. Showers are still in the forecast, especially in the southeast. However, because they are swift, they will not cause any inconvenience to tourists. By the way, July, not August, is the hottest month. The average temperature drops a few degrees in August, and there are fewer daylight hours. Summer evenings might be chilly, so a light jacket is recommended.

The coldest month in the UK in January, with wet snow and rain as precipitation. And towns are blanketed in fog, which is at its peak in the middle of winter. As a result, airports may freeze for a few days, causing all races to be cancelled. Winter is a time to snuggle up under a warm blanket with a cup of fragrant English tea rather than go sightseeing or participate in other activities.

Spring: In the United Kingdom, spring is all about new life sprouting after a long and difficult winter. In March, temperatures rise, frosts happen less often, and days get longer. Flowers sprout all over the place, trees shed their leaves, and animals reproduce. Spring in the UK is often rainy and breezy, so don't rush to buy sunglasses and flip-flops.

Spring is a season that begins in March and finishes in May, and it is one of the easiest to recognize as it transitions from winter to spring — the days grow longer and warmer. The weather in spring is usually calm and dry, yet there can be significant temperature changes between day and night because the ground hasn't had time to store any of the Sun's heat yet.

The sky is cloudy for the entire month of March. However, the weather in April brightens up at the beginning. The Sun appears more frequently, the air becomes warmer, and nature begins to bloom. Tourists start to arrive around the middle of April. In May, national parks, reserves, and other tourist attractions are already operating at total capacity. As a result, visitors may expect unexpected weather changes.

Summer: In the United Kingdom, summer should be hot and dry. In practice, it is only hot for brief periods, and most summers are still wet. Think of it as a strategy to make those hot summer days feel fabulous. Temperatures can reach 30°C on such days, albeit not much higher, and the British population takes advantage of it. People flock to the beaches, sit in parks, and generally enjoy the pleasant weather; this is mirrored by the increasing daylight hours, which reach over 17 hours in London in mid-June.

Summer has the warmest temperatures and the sunniest days. You may believe it is also the driest season, which it is at times, but rainfall varies significantly during the summer months, and this is when the UK has the most flooding. It begins in June and ends in August in the United States.

The summer solstice occurs when the northern hemisphere gets tilted towards the Sun. Every year on the 21st or 22nd of June, we have our longest day and shortest night.

Autumn is a transitional period between summer and winter and is likely to be the season with the most extreme weather conditions. September and perhaps even October can be hot and humid in the UK, with temperatures exceeding August. Conversely, November can sometimes be bitterly cold, occasionally with significant snowfall in the UK (like in 2010). Autumn is typically damp and windy, yet the weather is so changeable that it might feel like a different season from year to year.

Autumn begins in September and ends in November, during which time the weather becomes more remarkable, the weather gets stormier, and the days get shorter.

Rainfall becomes more frequent at the beginning of October, especially in the mountains. Fogs appear in the mornings, and heavy clouds cover the sky for the rest of the day. They emphasize the majesty of medieval fortresses. Due to the unpredictable state of British weather conditions, some days are sunny and peaceful. Because of the continuous rains, November is not the most fantastic month to visit Great Britain.

7.2.1 United Kingdom's Seasonal Activities
Activities differ with the seasons in the United Kingdom, as specific actions are restricted by the dominating season.

7.2.1.1 Activities to do in the winter
Snowboarding and skiing are two popular winter sports. Yes, skiing is now a pleasant reality in the Heart of England, which is recognized more for its lovely ancient houses than its quantity of snow. For example, the Snowdome in Tamworth Snow Centre in Hertfordshire has ski lifts and a mountain coated with real snow to slalom down the slopes without the stress of airports, travel delays, or extra baggage! So it's not surprising that this activity is one of the top winter pastimes in the United Kingdom.

If a manufactured setting isn't realistic enough for you, go to Aviemore in the Cairngorms, Scotland's ski capital, which comes alive as the winter snow blankets the country's rocky peaks. You may combine a ski trip with a cultural holiday to enjoy the rest of the Scottish Highlands, which is much cheaper than the alps.

7.2.1.2 Snowshoeing

Have you never heard of it before? On the other hand, Snowshoeing is a terrific way to experience the UK's snowy landscapes. Book a full-day or half-day guided trip in the Lake District, North Pennines, or Scotland with Eden Outdoor Adventures and enjoy the landscape, wildlife, and history along the route. Snowshoeing promises to be one of the best outdoor winter sports since it allows you to move across deep snow and access regions that standard footwear cannot.

7.2.1.3 Safari with reindeer during the Christmas season

Reindeer Lodge in Wales not only has a complete herd of reindeer to greet, but their particular winter drive-through safari offers a variety of festive events for the whole family to enjoy. In addition, a drive-in theatre show is available, and a lit lakeside and woodland trail to explore.

Little ones may extend the magic by visiting the hidden Elf Village, Santa's Grotto, and Toy Workshop. There's also a present for each youngster, carnival rides, Christmas stalls with various items, and seasonal hot food and drinks.

7.2.1.4 Sledging with dogs

While dog sledging is more prevalent in Scandinavian countries, that doesn't mean you can't participate in dog sledging activities here in the UK.

Arctic Quest in Gloucestershire, MynydSleddog Adventures in Wales, UK9 in Leicestershire, and Horse and Husky in Cumbria are just a few of the destinations in the UK that provide dog sledging, and all of them offer a wonderful experience, snow or no snow.

7.2.1.5 Natural hot springs in the wild

Did you know that the only hot springs in the UK feed the spas in Bath, Somerset? Spend a morning roaming through the historic city, learning how people used to relax and bathe in the past.

Escape the cold in the afternoon by booking a treatment at Thermae Bath Spa, where you can unwind in the open-air rooftop pool, float lazily in the warm waters of the Minerva Bath, and inhale the soothing scented vapours of the steam rooms; this happens to be one of the most relaxing winter hobbies available in the UK.

7.2.1.6 The English shore, catch some cold waves

Even in the dead of winter, the English coastline is ideal for catching waves, even if the water isn't as warm as it is in Bali or Australia. Surfers paddle out in the freezing ocean, even in the negative degrees, from snow or frost-covered beaches in search of monster waves and fewer competitors. When Arctic and Atlantic low-pressure systems build-up, the British coastline gets excellent waves, and surfers can catch their first major waves in September and into the winter months.

Beaches around the south coast, such as those at East and West Wittering, are good surf areas with lower waves than those along the Atlantic coast and surfing clubs that give introductory instruction. Surfers with more experience might check out the Atlantic coast of Cornwall and Devon, which has wild waves great for rides and tricks. Saunton Sands in Devon is an excellent place to go longboarding if you don't mind being alone on the beach with your friends.

If you prefer a more social atmosphere, Croyde Bay is one of the most popular surfing locations all year, offering lessons, rentals, and a vibrant hamlet where you can eat and socialize in the evening.

7.2.1.7 *In the Cairngorms, sleep in a snowhole*

In the Cairngorms, if you are digging a snow hole. You'll find additional creature amenities and artistic sculptures on a Northern Lights excursion in an Ice Hotel. A snowshoeing and mountain-walking expedition in the Scottish Cairngorms, on the other hand, will provide you with the joy of creating your own 'home' for the night.

The tour begins with winter skills instruction and a walk to the peak of CairnGorm. The more difficult adventure starts after a second comfortable night at the Fraoch Lodge.

Hikers carry a 10kg knapsack into the windy and snowy landscape, prepared for a night in the mountains. You can remove your wet gloves and relax after the hole is large enough to accommodate the entire expedition party.

7.2.2 Summary of summer activities

7.2.2.1 Dartmoor Bikepacking

Why not try bikepacking, the ultimate cycling and camping adventure? In Dartmoor National Park, a minimalist's dream, you may spend your days biking throughout the British countryside before sleeping in a local wild camping spot for a night immersed in nature under the stars.

7.2.2.2 Scrambling in a Welsh gorge

Those who prefer water-based activities will enjoy the opportunity to bathe in natural pools, go wild swimming, and climb over waterfalls when gorge climbing in Wales. So put on a wetsuit and helmet for this delightful summer pastime that allows you to enjoy magnificent clean waters, stunning scenery, and a heart-pounding adrenaline thrill.

7.2.2.3 Suffolk Sailboats

You can set out on the sailboat lifestyle and rent a modern yacht to explore the canals of The Broads for a more leisurely approach to taking to Britain's waters. There are a variety of attractive vessels to pick from, ranging from expensive yacht charters to humble wherries. Alternatively, try your hand at sailing by renting a sailboat in the Lake District's picturesque Ullswater.

7.2.2.4 Dorset coastal foraging

Beachgoers may take it a step further this summer by taking a seaweed foraging session along the Dorset coast to explore the fresh flavour of the British coast. The brand-new Seaweed Foraging, Wild Cooking & Feasting Course is an excellent introduction to the art of seaside foraging since it includes a beach walk, a foraged snack, a seaweed cooking workshop, and the opportunity to dine on the day's bounty in a three-course meal with wine.

7.2.2.5 Serpentine Park Nights

The annual event, which combines a variety of programs on art, dance, cinema, and technologies at the iconic Serpentine Pavilion designed by the renowned architect Francis Kéré, is a must-see for art fans.

The Park Nights series, which runs until the third weekend in September, comprises site-specific events by a diverse group of international artists, choreographers, and filmmakers.

7.2.2.6 Attend the London Carnival

The Notting Hill Carnival will feature 20 miles of colourful costumes and hundreds of Caribbean food booths on the August Bank Holiday weekend. At Emslie Horniman's Pleasance Park last Sunday, in August, there will be a Children Parade and Family Day and workshops.

7.2.2.7 GoBoat

Spend the afternoon on a boat on one of the city's rivers with your family. In Paddington, Kingston, and Canary Wharf, GoBoat offers private boat hire for groups of up to eight people. So what's the best part? The boats are composed of recyclable plastic and run-on electric engines, so you can enjoy your time on the lake without affecting the environment. In addition, it is not required to have any prior boating experience.

7.2.2.8 Take a wild swim

It is not much better than swimming in the sea, lake, or river on a hot summer day. There are plenty of wild swimming spots around London.

7.2.2.9 Take a bike ride

Peddle across the countryside with your tires pumped up. Cycling is a beautiful way to reconnect with nature and get away from the crowds. Take a walk along a local bike route, or if you're feeling more adventurous, go on a family bike packing trip somewhere nearby.

CHAPTER 8: CONCLUSION

Based on the prevalent concept that "good preparation prevents poor performance," it goes without saying that failing to organize your vacation to the United Kingdom properly will result in frustration, time and money waste, exhaustion, and dissatisfaction.

A weekend trip to the United Kingdom is the ideal antidote to the hectic work week. The days are long enough for you to stretch out and completely unwind. But not too brief to reap the benefits of a break from the routine. However, your trip and holiday could turn into another hectic and exhausting weekend without a guide to show you around.

On the other hand, this book provides valuable information and pointers to make things easier.

The first chapter of this book, About the United Kingdom, provides a comprehensive but quick overview of the geographical aspects of the United Kingdom, as well as covers and provides vital ecological and political information. Knowing that tourists must be well-versed in the country's culture, traditions, customs, weather conditions, language, and religious background to understand what to expect when they arrive at their destination in the United Kingdom.

The second part is an illustrated experiential guide on the activities, stunning monuments, and locations of the United Kingdom, which serves as a guide for every tourist on what to see, do, and the best accommodation options available in the United Kingdom. In addition, the chapter includes itineraries to help you make the most of your vacation time and money.

The third chapter provides essential and valuable travel information on aspects of the United Kingdom that you may not know, such as the best dinners, gorgeous museums, exciting castles, and spots.

Because we want you to enjoy the best vacation possible, the fourth chapter is filled with practical and easy survival suggestions, ranging from making reservations to beating the crowds in the United Kingdom and socializing with the locals.

Everything you need to know about golfing in the UK's unique cities is listed and explained here. The towns and attractive qualities are discussed in the fifth chapter.

Finally, your trip will be incomplete if you do not visit and participate in the numerous getaway activities and sites. This book would be unfinished without precise information about the seasons and their activities. These chapters cover vacation options in Great Britain and other cities, the best places to stay at your getaway destination, and everything there is to see and do there.

The purpose of this book is to assist you in discovering the United Kingdom and all of its features. Knowing that the book will be valuable to you while exploring, please leave a review and let us know how helpful this book has been.

REFERENCE

- History of Ancient Land Bridge Between Britain and Europe. 2000 Odufuwa Julius

- https://www.fs.fed.us/psw/publications/documents/gtr-181/004_Butler.pdf

- The Britons.Snyder, Christopher ISBN 978-0-631-22260-6

- Britain Begins. Oxford, UK: Oxford University Press. ISBN 978-0-19-967945-4.

- Checklist of the British & Irish Basidiomycota. Legon & Henrici

- The Jacobean Union: A Reconsideration of British Civil Policies Under the Early Stuarts, 1999. Nicholls, Andrew D.

- https://web.archive.org/web/20110813045413/http://pewresearch.org/pubs/896/global-anglicanism-at-a-crossroads

- https://www.gov.scot/publications/analysis-religion-2001-census/pages/2/

- An Atlas for Celtic Studies. Oxford: Oxbow Books. ISBN 978-1-84217-309-12007.Koch, John T.

- http://www.tara.tcd.ie/bitstream/handle/2262/40560/Edwards&Brooks_INJ08_TARA.pdf;jsessionid=68C65C0D09136670E8AEEF508E89031F?sequence=1

- https://golf.com/travel/best-worst-foods-eat-before-during-round-golf-2/

Printed in Great Britain
by Amazon

83606618R00078